THE COMPLETE GUIDE TO CARING FOR YOUR

CAT

CARE • NUTRITION • HEALTH & FIRST AID • BREEDS

THE COMPLETE GUIDE TO CARING FOR YOUR

CAT

Graham Meadows and Elsa Flint

BARNES
&NOBLE
BOOKS

NEW YORK

This edition published by Barnes & Noble, Inc. by arrangement
with New Holland Publishers (U.K.) Ltd

2004 by Barnes & Noble Books

M 10 9 8 7 6 5 4 3 2 1

ISBN 0-7607-5640-6

Publishing managers: Claudia Dos Santos / Simon Pooley
Designer: Richard MacArthur
Editor: Anna Tanneberger
Illustrations: Daniël van Vuuren
Picture researcher: Karla Kik
Production: Myrna Collins
Consultant: Rita Davis

Reproduction by Hirt & Carter (Cape) Pty Ltd
Printed and bound in Singapore by Kyodo Printing Co Pte Ltd

CONTENTS

Left: *Though they often seem remote and disinterested, cats are curious animals who like to keep well informed about their neighbourhood.*

1. CATS AND PEOPLE

▶ DOGS HAVE MASTERS. CATS HAVE STAFF. ANON. ◀

Those of us who are owned by cats may well subscribe to the theory that humans didn't domesticate the cat at all, but that the cat domesticated itself by walking into, adapting to and (in many cases) taking over people's lives. With few exceptions, the modern domestic cat remains independent and solitary, and has an undefinable wild streak. These cats have a look that says: 'I may live in your household, but don't expect me to conform.'

▶ THE ORIGIN OF THE DOMESTIC CAT ◀

A distant ancestor of today's domestic cat may have been Martelli's wild cat (*Felis lumensis*), a species now extinct. It was similar in size to today's small wild cats. About 600,000–900,000 years ago it may have given rise to *Felis silvestris*, from which three distinct species evolved, according to the regions and environments in which they lived. These were the central European or Forest wild cat (*F. silvestris silvestris*), the Asiatic desert cat (*F. silvestris ornata*) and the African wild cat (*F. silvestris lybica*). The latter inhabited most of Asia and North Africa and, because the process of domestication of the cat occurred mainly in the Middle East, the African wild cat was almost certainly the principal ancestor of modern domestic cats.

▶ DOMESTICATION ◀

For the cat, as for other domestic animals, the process of domestication occurred over a long period of time. Wild cats would have associated with humans only once the latter formed permanent settlements, grew grain crops, and set up grain stores. Grain stores would have attracted mice and rats, which in turn would have attracted wild cats.

Any sensible agriculturist would quickly have seen the advantage of encouraging the presence of these cats in order to help control the vermin and a loose, mutually beneficial association would have been forged.

Just when the process of domestication started is unclear though, and our estimates rely on archeological discoveries and the excavation of cat remains, which indicate a close association with humans. Although various cat remains have been found in Egyptian archeological sites dating back to 6700BC, there is no

Opposite: *Through their interaction with pets, children learn about love, death, and respect for other living creatures.*

CAT WORSHIP AND CULTURE

Many thousands of years ago a cat cult was well established in ancient Egypt. The feline goddess, Mafdet, was a snake-killer and protector of the pharaoh in the royal palace. Her pictures appear in magic formulas carved on pyramid chambers of the Fifth and Sixth Dynasties (before 2280BC).

The ancient Egyptians recognized the cat's role as a guardian of grain stores, and protected the animal by law. Sacred cats were also kept in their temples. In the temple of the cat goddess Bast or Pasht, from which the word 'puss' is said to have arisen, thousands of cats were mummified and laid in tombs. Excavations at other sites have also revealed large numbers of mummified cats, and the height of the cat cult is thought to have occurred at around 500BC, when many other animals were also a subject of worship. It was once thought that all the mummies were of household cats that had died from natural causes and whose remains had been presented to the temple by their mourning owners. More recently however, researchers have concluded that many of them were cats specially bred for sacrifice, because they had died from a broken neck and many were merely kittens.

firm evidence that these were necessarily domesticated animals, and they are more likely to have been wild cats. If you accept that finding a cat skeleton buried with a person is evidence that the cat was domesticated, then a 7000-year-old burial site at Mostagedda, in Egypt, is evidence enough. There, excavations revealed a man buried with two animals at his feet: a cat and a gazelle.

If this doesn't convince you, then you need to move forward 2500 years – to the earliest depiction of cats in Egyptian tomb art. As further evidence, cat remains recovered from an archeological site in the Indus Valley in Asia, dating back to 2000BC, could well be from a domesticated variety, and paintings and inscriptions from the same period portray cats in situations that suggest that they were domesticated.

From that time on there is plenty of evidence to show that cats became well established in Egyptian homes. A painting at Thebes, in the tomb of the harbor master, May, and his wife Tui (dated around 1600BC), portrays a ginger cat sitting beneath Tui's chair. It wears a collar, and its leash is tied to a chair leg. The inference is that it was a pet, although this could be disputed.

A picture in the tomb of someone named Baket (dated around 1500BC) depicts a house attendant watching a cat that is eyeing a rat. Other tombs in Thebes also contain paintings of cats. One of them, dated at 1400BC, depicts a

Top: *Cats were worshipped in ancient Egypt, and many were mummified to accompany their owners into the next world.*

kitten sitting on the lap of the sculptor Ipuy. There are also some interesting, though inconclusive, artifacts to suggest that by this period in history cats were not only kept as pets in homes, but also used to help people hunt. At least three tomb paintings, one of them in the tomb of the sculptor Nebuman (around 1400BC), show cats apparently participating in the action while wildfowlers are using throwing sticks to catch and kill ducks and other birds. Were these cats helping to flush out game from the reed beds and/or helping to retrieve it? A skeptic might suggest that they were simply there to take advantage of a free lunch.

THE TAMING OF THE CAT

It has been suggested that during the process of domestication, a genetic change to the wild temperament (a 'domestication mutation') must have occurred to reduce the wild cat's innate aggression and make domestication possible. The basis for this reasoning is that in wild cats tameness (lack of aggression) is not inherited. Although individual animals can be tamed, their kittens are born with a wild temperament and in their turn must also be tamed. In the domestic cat, kittens inherit tameness from their mother – therefore, the reasoning goes, some genetic change must have occurred in the domestic cat to cause this.

The idea of a domestication mutation is intriguing, for its exponents suggest that when this occurs it prevents the development of certain adult behavior patterns, with the result that adult animals still retain some juvenile behaviors. Retaining these behaviors makes them better suited to domestication. The term for this is neoteny, and it functions as follows:

Above: *A lioness (Panthera leo) is forever vigilant, watching for potential danger to her cubs, even when they are no longer tiny and hopelessly vulnerable.*

In the wild, adult cats are solitary. A close-knit 'family' group is formed when a female gives birth to and rears her kittens, but once the kittens become independent there is no continuing association, and each individual becomes a 'loner'.

Domestic cats, on the other hand, behave rather differently. They are more gregarious, and the suggestion is that this is because they retain some of their 'kittenish' instinct to stick together. There are several examples to demonstrate this. If the owner of a female cat that has given birth to kittens decides to keep one or more of those kittens once they have been reared, the mother and offspring will often form close family bonds.

Even when domestic cats are feral, their families tend to stay together. In urban areas, where there are comparatively dense domestic cat populations, unrelated adults will often form loose associations. Groups of them may even meet together at certain times of the day for 'cat conferences', which seem to be the cat equivalent of humans 'hanging out' together.

Neoteny could arise from a genetic mutation, but it could also result from the process of human selection. People would choose to keep and breed the cats that were the easiest to manage. Those displaying juvenile characteristics were more family-oriented and less independent than adults, and therefore more suited to life within a human family.

Neoteny is not just a characteristic of domestic cats. It occurs in domestic dogs, too, where adults retain certain puppy characteristics that make it easier to integrate them into a human family.

Whether such a genetic change occurred and if so, when we shall never know. We can only surmise that people kept the kittens of wild cats, and that some of these (probably females) proved tame enough to keep to adulthood and breed. Eventually, for various reasons, kittens were born that were less aggressive and more suited to living with humans.

Nevertheless, the domestic cat's wild temperament is only just below the surface, and not all cats show the same degree of 'tameness'. There is a wide range of temperaments within the domestic cat population – some cats are extremely tame and others have a definite wild streak. Also, lack of aggression in domestic cats needs to be reinforced by human contact from an early age. If it is not, some of the cat's wild attributes reappear. For example, kittens born to a domestic cat that has gone feral are distrustful of humans. They need to be subjected to at least a basic taming process before they will adapt to living in a human home.

Top right: *Cats are remarkably agile, and are powerful and accurate jumpers.*
Above: *The origin of the Russian Blue is uncertain. It is said that sailors brought specimens back to Britain from the northern Russian port of Archangel.*

CATS AND PEOPLE

THE SPREAD OF CATS

As more trade routes developed between countries around the Mediterranean and in Asia, the spread of domestic cats also grew. Around 900BC, Phoenician traders took them to Italy. From there they spread slowly across the rest of Europe, during which time genes from the European wild cat were introduced (by accident, design, or both).

We know that cats had arrived in England by AD1000, during the period of early Viking settlement. The evidence for this is that cat remains have been discovered at several archeological sites dating from that period (including the ancient Viking village of Jorvik, in York, England).

All these cats were shorthaired, but further to the east, longhaired varieties were being developed. It has been suggested that the gene for long hair may have come from the Manul (*Felis manul*) of central Asia, but it is more likely to have originated from artificial

selection for the gene that produces long hair. The gene for long hair spread from southern Russia into Pakistan, Turkey and Iran, and eventually showed up in the Angora and Persian breeds. Longhaired varieties arrived in Italy from Turkey during the 16th century. That was also about the time when the Manx cat arrived in the Isle of Man, brought in from the Far East by Spanish traders, who regularly plied those routes.

The first colonists took shorthaired cats with them when they emigrated to the New World, and later settlers took a vast variety of cats with them to Australia and New Zealand. Domestic cats are now found all over the world.

Top right: *Blue eyes are the most striking feature of the Siamese cat.*
Above: *Today there are more than 160 color varieties in the Persian breed.*

COAT COLORS AND PATTERNS

Some of the coat colors and patterns in domestic cats are thought to be very old, because they have had time to spread all over the world. They include black, blue (a slate-gray color which is a 'diluted' form of black) and orange (ginger). The Siamese and Burmese color patterns, on the other hand, are more recent and originated in southeast Asia – where they were preserved and spread because of human preference.

Some color patterns spread of their own accord. For example, hundreds of years ago in Britain, the blotched tabby appears to have arisen as a mutation of the striped tabby. For reasons yet to be fully explained, it appears that the blotched tabby and black cat are better able to thrive in a high-density urban environment. In some areas (especially in England) these colors are becoming predominant among alley cats and non-pedigree domestic cats.

▶ BREEDING ◀

By their very nature, cats are free-ranging animals. Mature males (known as toms) especially, are wanderers. Before the concept of selective breeding began about 150 years ago, this wanderlust in domestic cats provided plenty of opportunity for the intermingling of genes. If there were two distinct races of cat in any region, they blended over a period time, and this means we cannot be sure of the origin of many of our modern domestic breeds.

Nevertheless, studies of the skeletal structure, body type and hair length of modern breeds enable us to make an informed guess.

The heavier, more thickset body type, found in British Shorthairs and Persians, shows the influence of the European wild cat. The foreign and Oriental breeds (such as the Abyssinian and Siamese) retain the lithe body of the African wild cat.

There seems to be no evidence for the claim that some domestic breeds (such as the Angora, Chinese cat and Siamese) have an Asiatic origin and may be descended from Pallas's cat (*Otocolobus manul*) or its close relatives; the skulls of these cats show no similarity to the Asiatic species.

Top: *Most, but not all, ginger cats are male. This is because the color of the coat is determined by a sex-linked gene.*

THE DEVELOPMENT OF PEDIGREE BREEDS

It was not until the middle of the 19th century that the idea of selective breeding and recording of pedigree cats took hold in Britain and Europe. Some breeders started their breeding programs using ordinary shorthaired 'moggies', selecting them for their body shape and coat color. From these humble ancestors, over the years and through selective breeding, today's British and European Shorthair breeds were created.

In the United States, the foundation stock for shorthairs also came from local cats. These were the descendants of the cats brought over by the early settlers 200 years earlier, which had developed quite distinctive characteristics of their own. These are now reflected in the American Shorthair.

During the early days of cat breeding there were already longhaired domestic cats, but the main development of the pedigree longhair breeds came initially from the Angora cat, which had originated in Turkey, and later from other longhair breeds imported from Persia and Afghanistan. Both the latter types quickly became known as Persians. Their popularity grew at the expense of the Angora, which almost disappeared from the breeding scene.

By the late 19th century, exports and imports of pedigree cats were starting in earnest, and by the end of the century the Siamese, Russian Blue, and Abyssinian had already reached Britain.

During the 20th century the export and import of cats continued. The first Birman arrived in France in 1919, and the ancestor of the modern Burmese entered the United States from Rangoon in 1930.

During the 1950s the Egyptian Mau and Korat reached the United States, and Turkish cats were brought into Britain. The Japanese Bobtail arrived in the United States in 1968, and the 1970s brought the Angora and Singapura. Some time later Maine Coons arrived in Australia, where the Spotted Mist was developed, and Ocicats entered New Zealand.

The spread of pedigree cats – and also the development of new breeds or color varieties – continues throughout the world. There are now dozens of different breeds and hundreds of different color varieties of cats.

Above: *Don't be surprised to hear your mother cat purring loudly when she suckles her kittens.*

▶ CAT SHOWS ◀

The first recorded cat show was held at St Giles Fair, Winchester, England, in 1598. During the 19th century, as cats increased in popularity, shows also became more popular. At the earliest events cats were brought along and shown in a variety of containers, or even in their owner's arms. The cat show as we know it today originated from an idea by an Englishman called Harrison Weir, who decided to house and display cats in rows of cages on benches or tables. His first show, called the National Cat Show, was held in 1871 at the Crystal Palace in London, and at least 160 cats were displayed. This type of display became known as a 'benched' show, a name that is still used today.

Cat shows are now regular events and an integral part of the pedigree cat scene. However, more and more shows are including a section for non-pedigree cats, thereby attracting ordinary cat owners to display their pets and in turn view the pedigree entries. These shows increase the public's awareness of advances in the pedigree world, known as the Cat Fancy.

Above: *Cat shows are an ideal venue to familiarize yourself with the characteristics of different breeds. Cats are judged on their condition, their head shape, coat, eye color, and shape, and even their tails.*

CATS AND PEOPLE

THE CAT FANCY

During the late 19th century, as interest in breeding and showing increased, it became clear that there was a need for some form of control, and for the official recognition and recording of different breeds. In 1887 the National Cat Club, the first organization of its kind, was formed in Britain, with Harrison Weir as its president. It instituted a stud book and set up a system for the official registration of pedigree cats. This organization later amalgamated with another to become the Governing Council of the Cat Fancy (GCCF). In 1983 a further registering body was set up in Britain: the Cat Association of Britain (CAB).

The first registering body in the United States was the American Cat Association (ACA), established in 1899. Still in existence, it is one of several organizations in operation in the country. The Cat Fanciers' Association (CFA) maintains the largest American registry of cats, and is also the largest registry of cats in the world.

BREED STANDARDS

Most countries now have at least one governing body (and some have several) to oversee the recognition and registration of cat breeds and to set the standards for each of them. In each country these standards are outlined in special publications that are regularly reviewed and provide guidelines for breeders and judges.

Not all organizations recognize the same breeds or classify them in the same way, and breed standards can vary markedly between countries. The biggest variations occur in the United States.

Top right: *This sorrel Abyssinian, a breed that does not like being confined, is clearly an old hand at cat shows.*
Above: *Judges examine a British Sealpoint at a show. They award points for certain characteristics that are defined in the breed's standard. Deviations, such as a kink in the tail, for instance, would immediately disqualify the cat.*

▶ CATS AND PEOPLE ◀

In modern society the companionship of pet animals are one of the many factors that make up what we call 'quality of life'.

During the last 20 years, numerous studies have confirmed the psychological and medical benefits of pet ownership. These benefits have become the basis for programs developed around animal-assisted activities (AAA) and animal-assisted therapy (AAT). Also known as 'pet-facilitated therapy' and 'animal-facilitated therapy', these programs involve interactions between animals and humans to assist people with physical or psychological problems.

Animal-assisted activities are informal 'meet and greet' programs in which progress is not measured or documented. Examples are taking pets to visit the elderly in nursing homes and hospitals, and the use of pets to help relieve loneliness and isolation in specific groups such as abused children, prisoners, and persons in various forms of therapy.

Animal-assisted therapy is based on a formal program that sets out to achieve a target, and is documented by a professional in the field of health or human services. This person may be a physician, occupational therapist, physical therapist, certified therapeutic recreation specialist, teacher, nurse, social worker, speech therapist, or mental-health professional. The animal may be handled by the professional, or by a volunteer under the direction of a professional. The aim of the program may be improvement in social skills, range of motion, verbal skills, or attention span, for example.

Above: *At seven weeks, kittens such as these are fully weaned and eating solid foods, happy to interact with people, and ready to go to a new home.*

Each session is documented in the person's record with the progress and activity noted.

For example, an occupational therapist may, with the assistance of a cat and its handler, devise a routine to increase the range of motion in a person's arm. By making the effort to stroke or hold the cat the arm's mobility and range of motion is improved. The progress made during each session is documented by the occupational therapist.

In industrialized societies, increasing affluence, a falling birth rate, and looser family ties have resulted in pets playing an even more important psychological role. Many more couples are choosing not to have children, or to have them much later in life, when the female partner has had time to establish her career. For many of these people a pet becomes an important member of the family. But whatever the composition of your human family, owning a cat or two is likely to provide you with some important benefits.

COMPANIONSHIP

For the majority of cat owners this is the most important feature of cat ownership. It is enough simply to have the cat living in the same house, as a partner, a friend, or a fellow living creature. It is not unusual for people to talk to cats, and for the cat to respond with vocalizations. As well as talking to cats, humans instinctively use methods of communication that they would use with other humans. To console them, we use standard 'primate gestures' such as stretching out our hands and stroking them, pursing and smacking our lips and 'soft-voicing'.

COMFORT, SUPPORT AND RELAXATION

You may derive comfort either from the affection that your cat displays towards you, or from direct physical contact, such as when your cat rubs up against you, or when you stroke it, or when it lies on your lap.

People need comforting when they feel sad or depressed, and a cat can certainly help cheer them up. This aspect is particularly relevant to younger family members in times of trouble. If a teenager is going through a difficult period in his or her life, a cat can provide much-needed emotional support.

Your cat will certainly help you relax. It has been conclusively demonstrated that a person in a state of tension shows a slowing of the heart rate and a drop in blood pressure when their pet comes on the scene. Owning a pet is an important stress-management practice for people with high stress levels.

A cat can also provide psychological protection. For example, it can give a person the emotional security to face or overcome irrational fears, such as fear of the dark or anxiety at being left alone.

Top: *Despite their reputation for aloofness, it is not unusual for a cat to head-butt and lick its owner to show affection.*

HELPING TO ESTABLISH NEW FRIENDSHIPS

There is plenty of evidence to show that people who like animals are more likely to like other people, and to be more socially interactive. If you own a cat you are probably good at establishing new human friendships, and are unlikely to allow your cat to become a substitute for, or even a distraction from, relationships with other people.

Cats can certainly act as catalysts for contact between humans, and can also serve as an important link between the young and the old.

SELF-FULFILMENT AND SELF-ESTEEM

We all need to feel good about ourselves. Many of us achieve this through success in our family relationships, work, sport or other recreational activities. Others achieve it through the ownership of or by breeding a cat that is an object of admiration. It may be a winner in the show ring, or a rare or unusual breed. But your cat doesn't have to be a show winner - every common cross-breed has its own, unique character and appearance, and you will experience a deep sense of satisfaction simply by looking at it and knowing that it is yours.

For some of us the mere responsibility of caring for another living creature can result in a sense of self-worth, and by doing it correctly we may be rewarded by the approval of other people as well.

AN AID TO LEISURE ACTIVITIES

Cats are an important part of our leisure experience. They like to play, and they stimulate us to play with them and to experience joy. This helps us to relax and develop a more active zest for life, diverting us from the comparative drudgery of household chores or work. For many of us, merely looking after a cat i.e. feeding and grooming it - can become a leisure activity in itself.

BENEFITS TO CHILDREN

The majority of families that own a cat also have children. We might ask ourselves why parents coping with a growing family would want to saddle themselves with another, non-human member, and the answer is not entirely clear. Many of us think that having a pet cat will help teach our children responsibility; that a child who learns to respect and care for a pet is more likely to have a caring attitude towards fellow humans.

There is also an educational value. If our children learn about a cat's body processes and how

Above: *The Siamese is an extrovert, people-oriented cat that loves human company – it may even be taught to walk on a leash.*

CATS AND PEOPLE

to cope with its health problems or illness, they may be better prepared for their own experiences later in life. The life cycle of a pet cat averages about 15 years, and may match the period during which children grow to maturity. The life of a cat might help to teach children about growing up, learning, old age, suffering, and death. Caring for it during these times may teach them some valuable 'parenting' skills.

The presence of a cat in your household can help your children to overcome anxiety, control aggression, develop self-awareness and deal with the problems that occur in life.

Research has shown that when their parents or siblings aren't around, children will often talk to the family cat about the day's successes or failures. It is interesting to note that the children most likely to develop social skills and empathy with other people are those who talk intimately and at length with their pets and their grandparents.

THERAPEUTIC VALUE

Your cat will probably bring you plenty of other benefits as well. Statistically you are likely to:

- live longer
- have lower blood pressure
- be in less danger of suffering heart attacks
- suffer less stress and be more likely to gain relief from tension
- be emotionally stronger and less likely to become depressed
- be less aggressive
- have better motivation, and be more likely to be goal-oriented and purposeful
- be less self-centered and more supportive of others
- be less judgmental of other people.

BETTER HOUSEKEEPING

It has been shown that families with pets of any kind are generally more hygiene conscious than families without pets.

BENEFITS TO THE ELDERLY

Cats can be of special benefit to elderly people who often fail to feed themselves properly. Feeding a cat stimulates the owner to eat, too, and a cat provides the elderly with company while they are eating.

Elderly people moving into retirement homes would certainly benefit if they could take their pet cat with them, but this is often impractical. For this reason some retirement homes keep one or more cats for the benefit of the residents.

Top: *An ever-present reminder to relax – a cat's ability to let go and take it easy, yet remain alert is the envy of every stressed, over-worked cat owner.*

2. YOUR NEW CAT

▶ CHOOSING YOUR FELINE COMPANION ◀

Like most people, you may find yourself choosing your own cat, but don't rule out the possibility that your cat will choose you. You will be walking past a pet shop or veterinary clinic and there, peering out at you, will be an adorable little cat face with pleading eyes. You have been thinking about a cat, but not too seriously. Now here is this bundle of fluff, asking you to give it a home. It will be difficult to resist.

Some stray cats have the routine worked out, too. They turn up on a doorstep, get to know the premises, check out the standard of meal service, win over the human inhabitant(s) and then, before you know it, they will have moved in.

Although some neighborhood cats do choose their owners in one of the above ways, most are selected following a planned and carefully considered decision on the part of their owners.

▶ FACTORS TO CONSIDER ◀

○ Why do you want a cat? Is it to become a companion, is it for breeding purposes or do you want to enter it in shows?

○ What other animals do you have already, and will a cat integrate with them?

○ Is your property suitable for the type of cat you envisage? A small, high-rise apartment may suit a lethargic domestic longhair, but will be inadequate for an active Oriental. A house bordering a busy highway could guarantee a short lifespan and a great deal of heartache for you.

○ Who will look after it? Even if it is a family pet, you should make sure that one person takes on the responsibility of feeding the cat a proper diet and ensuring that the cat receives the correct vaccinations at the right intervals and is regularly dewormed and treated for fleas. Don't rely on children's promises. When children are too young for the responsibility, later in life pet ownership may only hold bad memories for them.

○ How will it integrate with the other animals in your household? Will the family terrier terrorize it? Will an incumbent cat consider the new one an interloper and try to drive it away? Is your favorite budgie likely to become a cat's dinner? Will the goldfish in your garden pond continue to lead their current peaceful life?

○ Can you afford it? Cats may be cheaper to feed than dogs, but they still require health care. This can be costly.

○ Is any member of the family an asthmatic? Many asthmatics are allergic to cat fur, so do your homework.

Opposite: *Without a care in the world – cats leave many of life's responsibilities up to you!*

▸ WHERE TO BUY YOUR CAT ◂

Animal shelters and rescue organizations usually have a selection of cats of varying ages. Many of them employ veterinarians who check the animals' health before they are advertised for a home, and cats from such a source will usually have been vaccinated prior to sale.

Veterinary clinics are another reliable source. Many of them have clients who are looking for a good home for a cat or kittens. These animals will probably have been subjected to health checks, and the veterinary staff will ensure that they receive their proper vaccinations. Pet stores commonly have kittens for sale. If you are buying a cat from such a source, do so only if the store agrees that purchase is conditional on the cat passing a veterinary health check. If the cat or kitten has not been vaccinated, get this done as soon as possible.

If you decide to get a kitten or cat by answering an advertisement, also only take the animal on condition that it passes a veterinary health check.

Occasionally a kitten or cat may arrive as a (welcome) gift, and in this case the giver should have taken all necessary steps to ensure that the animal is healthy.

Above: *Too many kittens are left homeless and have to be destroyed. If you can, get your new cat from an animal welfare center such as this one.*

▶ PEDIGREE OR NON-PEDIGREE? ◀

If you are interested in showing and/or breeding, then a pedigree cat may be the right way for you to go. If showing your cat is what interests you, rather than the complications of breeding, remember that most cat shows have classes for non-pedigree animals, so you don't have to own a pedigree cat in order to be able to show it.

PEDIGREE CATS

Depending on where you live, you may have a choice of 40 or more pedigree breeds, ranging from longhaired cats such as the Chinchilla to sleek shorthairs like the British Shorthair or the Foreign (also called the Oriental). If you prefer something rather different, you can opt for a Norwegian Forest Cat, a Turkish Van or a LaPerm. Within some of the breeds (such as the longhairs and Persians) there is a wide range of coat colors, perhaps as many as 50. There are plenty of books and Internet sites that list and describe these breeds and varieties, so if you are thinking of getting one of them, do your homework first.

Remember, too, to talk to your veterinarian. Vets get to see many of the health and behavioral problems that arise in the local cat population, and have a good idea of any pitfalls. They know which breeders are reputable and which are not, and while they may not be willing to name the latter they can certainly steer you clear of them.

One advantage of choosing a pedigree animal is that you should be able to get a good idea of what the mother, and possibly also the father, is like. Reputable breeders are happy for you to visit them and inspect their animals for temperament and health. Avoid breeders who make excuses, won't let you view the parents, and won't give you sufficient information.

Just as individual cats vary in their temperament, so do the various breeds. For example, some longhairs (such as Persians) are friendly, comparatively inactive and enjoy nothing more than a cuddle on a warm lap. Others tend to be rather aloof and object to too much handling. The Siamese and Foreign (Oriental) breeds are far more demanding and independent. Don't confuse such perfectly normal 'cat attitude' with poor temperament, though, which is often expressed as aggression. Some pedigree animals have a very poor temperament, caused through selection for their physical appearance with regard to little else, so watch out for it and don't select an animal that comes from such stock.

Cats that have obvious physical defects, such

Above: *The Korat is a very old breed, native to Thailand (where it is known as the Si-Sawat).*
Top: *Cats spend a large part of their day fastidiously grooming themselves, and can reach almost every part of their fur with their tongues. This breed is an Oriental Red Lynx.*

as in-turned eyelids (particularly prevalent in some Persian and exotic varieties) should also be avoided. If a breeder tells you that this condition is normal for the breed, be wary, because while runny eyes or labored breathing may be acceptable to some breeders, both of these conditions are a potential health problem. If you are in any doubt, talk to your veterinarian first, or purchase the animal subject to a health check.

NON-PEDIGREE CATS

The majority of pet cats are of unknown pedigree, and if you choose such an animal the chances are that you will be unable to obtain much information about its ancestry. You may be able to see its mother and get some idea of her character, but that won't necessarily give you an indication as to how her offspring will turn out. Every cat is an individual, and this particularly applies to the non-pedigree or 'domestic' types. What you see is what you get. Having said that, the vast majority of non-pedigree cats turn out to be ideal household companions. Their ancestors had to be tough, sensible, adaptable, and healthy in order to survive, endowing their offspring with what scientists call hybrid vigor: a mixture of genes that gives an individual cat a good chance of surviving and reproducing.

▶ KITTEN OR ADULT? ◀

Many non-pedigree kittens are offered for homes from six to eight weeks of age. At this age they should have been properly weaned and socialize well into their new homes. They still need toilet training, and are unlikely to have had any vaccinations.

By contrast, responsible pedigree breeders will not usually allow their kittens to go to a new home until they are at least 12 weeks old. By this time they are house-trained and have received their first course of vaccinations.

A kitten may be far more appealing than an adult, and may fulfill your need to nurture a young animal. You will have less idea of what its temperament will eventually be, but the way

Top: *If you want a pedigree kitten, make sure you get one from a reputable breeder, and involve the whole family in your selection process.*

a kitten is handled and brought up will influence its character and, properly treated, the vast majority of kittens turn out be ideal cat companions.

When deciding between kitten and adult, do remember that animal shelters have juvenile and adult cats waiting for, and deserving of, good homes. Some pedigree adults become surplus to breeders' requirements and, after neutering, are available as pets. It is easier to determine the temperament of an adult cat.

▶ CHOOSING THE SEX ◀

If you are buying a pedigree cat and hoping to breed, then you will probably choose a female. A stud cat (male) usually needs to be kept in separate quarters and, because of its scent-marking, rarely makes a good family pet. If you do not intend to breed, then sex is not really an issue because, as a responsible pet owner, you should arrange to have the kitten (or, if necessary, the adult cat) neutered. There is little difference in the behavior of a neutered male and a neutered female, and both sexes can make an adorable, loving pet.

▶ CHOOSING THE INDIVIDUAL ◀

Look for a healthy kitten or cat whose temperament and personality suits you and your lifestyle. To get an idea of which individual might be suitable, you need to spend some time with it. If you are with an adult cat, sit with it and talk to it, and see how it relates to you. Gauge its reaction to being touched or handled. If you are with a litter of kittens, handle each kitten in turn. A kitten that is unduly shy, or excessively aggressive towards its littermates may continue to exhibit those traits in adult life, although that is not always

Top: *Adult cats have less of a chance of finding a new home than kittens do, yet they can be the ideal choice for an elderly person who does not wish to cope with an energetic kitten.*
Center: *Play fighting is an important part of the kitten's mental and physical development, where the animals learn to attack others and defend themselves.*

the case. If the kittens' mother is present while you are with them, check her temperament and health as well.

When investigating a cat or kitten for health and temperament, use the following checklist:

- It readily approaches you and does not back away or show aggression.
- It is alert, bright, gentle, and playful, and not dull or lethargic.
- It holds its head normally, and walks or runs without limping.
- No head shaking, sneezing, or coughing.
- The skin appears clean and healthy, without sores, scabs, dirt, or flea droppings. The fur is glossy, clean, and well groomed, with no areas of hair loss or matting.
- There are no discharges from the eyes, nose, or ears. The third eyelid (nictitating membrane) is not partly covering the eyeball.
- The teeth appear clean and free of tartar. The gums are a healthy salmon-pink color and show no signs of bleeding.
- The belly feels reasonably firm and is not distended. It is neither too hard nor too flabby.

- The anus is clean, and there are no visible signs of diarrhea or tapeworm segments (which emerge from the anus and look like grains of rice).
- Details of the existing diet are available.

If you don't feel competent to make the above assessments, take somebody along with you who is. If even one member of a litter of kittens appears unhealthy, you would be wise to choose from another source.

Once you have decided on an individual, make sure that it has been sexed correctly.

Finally, ask for a 10 to 14-day approval period during which you can obtain an independent health check from your veterinarian. Any infections that are incubating will show up during this time.

If you have purchased a pedigree cat or kitten, make sure that you receive the correct registration papers. If one of the conditions of purchase is that the cat or kitten must be neutered (desexed), then it is normal practice for the breeder to withhold such papers until after you provide proof that the operation has been performed.

▶ ONE OR TWO? ◀

Many people think in terms of one kitten or cat, but do consider the option of taking two together. Cats certainly enjoy solitude on occasions, but they are also communal animals and two individuals will often prove good company for each other while their human owners are away from home at the office.

Above: *Kittens that have had very little or no contact with humans may be distrustful and difficult to socialize.*

▶ INTEGRATING A NEW CAT WITH EXISTING PETS ◀

Before you bring a second (or even a third) cat into your household, you should make sure you are familiar with cat behavior both with regards to territorial behavior and aggression, and the basic principles of cat training (*see pp72–85*). Some cats will accept a newcomer, especially a kitten (which may be perceived as less of a threat), but others will not.

You will help this integration by gradually introducing the newcomer to your cat(s), keeping it separated in one room until it has gained confidence (especially if it is a kitten) and your existing cats have become used to it. The newcomer is probably unsure and may be frightened as it is moving into new and unfamiliar territory which is already occupied (and may be defended) by the current feline

Top: *Goldfish and small mammals that are kept as pets need to be protected from the family cat – make sure their cages are secure, and avoid keeping a goldfish in an open bowl.*
Above: *Cats and kittens may not usually like water, but they enjoy stalking its inhabitants.*

inhabitants. Feed them separately to reduce competition for food, and make a fuss of your existing cats so that they do not feel neglected because of the new arrival.

If you already own a dog, the introductory process is similar to that described above – gradual and non-threatening. Once again, the dog may immediately accept the cat. Sometimes a bitch will accept a kitten and relate to it rather like the way she would to one of her own pups, even to the extent of offering it some protection. Make sure that you give the incumbent dog as much fuss and attention as usual (or even more), and praise and reward it for good behavior.

Introducing a new cat to pet birds can pose a problem. If it is a kitten purchased from a breeder, it may never have experienced the sight or stimulation that a bird presents. Although its basic hunting or playing instinct may cause it to react, it may be quite easy to train your cat to ignore the bird or even to accept it as a companion. If, however, it is a kitten from a domestic cat that has had the opportunity to introduce its kittens to bird prey, or is an adult cat that has already learned to catch birds, then you have a more difficult task on your hands. If you find that you do have such a problem, talk to your veterinarian.

Goldfish are yet another pet that can be threatened by an incoming cat. Those kept indoors in an aquarium tank with a glass lid and artificial lighting should be safe, but any that are exposed to an inquisitive cat may stimulate an unwanted reaction. Goldfish in an outdoor pond are also susceptible to a cat's attentions, and you may need to train your cat to leave them alone. Protective measures include physical barriers such as netting, and the installation of plenty of water plants - such as water lilies – under which the fish can hide.

Top: *Dogs, especially bitches, may willingly accept and mother kittens in the household.*

YOUR NEW CAT

► INTRODUCING A CAT TO CHILDREN ◄

If you have a baby, you are more likely to want to protect it from the cat. Make sure that the cat cannot climb into a young baby's crib, because there is always the danger that the cat will jump down onto the baby's face and scratch it, or curl up close to the baby's face and obstruct its breathing.

Toddlers can cause a new cat some problems, because they tend to want to hold the animal – usually in extremely uncomfortable, if not painful, positions. You need to train your child just as much as your cat to ensure that they both get the most enjoyment from each other.

The same applies to older children, especially if this is the first pet they have experienced. They need to understand how the newcomer feels, and the importance of keeping it free from stress and allowing it some time out on its own. Children have similar needs, and it shouldn't be too difficult for them to learn to treat the new cat as an individual rather than an object or toy.

Above: *When choosing a new kitten, try to view the whole litter at home. Although the smallest kitten may look cute, it is more likely to be weak and sickly. The boldest, biggest kitten is a better choice.*

3. CARING FOR YOUR CAT

▶ A NEW CAT, A NEW HOME ◀

Ideally every cat should live in the home of a caring and informed owner, but many cats are left to fend for themselves or are treated as dispensable items that can be left behind when the owner moves out. If you regard owning a cat as a privilege, not a right, then you will help to create the happy and satisfying mutual relationship that so many cat owners have experienced.

Remember that your cat's temperament, enjoyment of life, health, and welfare are influenced by the way you and your family treat it. Properly cared for, your cat can bring you happiness and provide you with affection and loyalty. Many cats eagerly await their owner's return home at the end of the day. Some will accompany their owner on an evening walk. Some even show their appreciation by bringing home prey and presenting it to their favorite person. Yes, believe it or not, cats can indeed be loyal to their owner.

▶ A CAT BED AND BEDDING ◀

It is possible to purchase a wide variety of manufactured plastic or wooden cat beds, wicker baskets or bean bags, and washable wool or synthetic rugs.

If you want something cheap but effective, an old cardboard box with one side partly cut away to make an entrance will prove perfectly adequate. Line the box with newspaper and place a piece of washable blanket on top of the paper. Remember, though, that a cardboard box cannot be properly cleaned and will need to be replaced from time to time.

Place the bed in a quiet, draft-free corner away from family traffic so that the cat can have some privacy when it so chooses. If you have a spare room, lend this to your new cat for a week or two until it has grown used to your household and its activities.

Above: *Even though your cat will enjoy sleeping on your bed or any cushion or chair, it should have a bed of its own to provide it with a sense of security.*
Opposite: *When you hold your cat, always keep one hand under its hindquarters for support.*

▶ A LITTERBOX AND CAT LITTER ◀

It is very important that a cat litterbox should be easy to clean. Some trays have disposable liners. Newspapers serve the same purpose, but they need to be changed at frequent intervals or they will start to smell. It is usually best to use a commercial cat litter that contains absorbent clay material or Fuller's earth – substances that absorb the odors of urine and feces. You can find cat litter that is made of bark, but it is not as effective.

Place the litterbox in a quiet corner, as far as possible from the cat's bed and its food: cats will not use the litterbox in an area close to where they eat.

▶ FEEDING UTENSILS ◀

Food and water dishes must be either washable or disposable. You can use disposable plastic dishes or one of the many types of plastic or pottery bowl. Plastic dispensers for dry food and drinking water are ideal once a kitten or cat has learned to use them. Whichever type of utensil you choose, it is important to clean or change them regularly.

▶ GROOMING GEAR ◀

Basic equipment is comprised of double-sided body brush, a coarse comb and a fine (flea) comb. If you have a longhaired cat you may require additional equipment to keep it groomed, such as a pair of blunt-ended scissors for cutting away sections of a matted coat. If you're an eager groomer, keep a chamois leather cloth, which can be used to polish your shorthair's coat.

Above: *A grooming tool for every coat type – rubber brushes, wire bristle brushes and fine- and wide-toothed combs.*

CARING FOR YOUR CAT

▶ COLLAR ◀

If you want your cat to wear a collar with an identification tag or a bell (the idea of which is to warn garden birds of the cat's presence), attach it only once your cat has settled into its new home. The collar must have an elastic section so that, if the cat gets caught by the collar, the elastic will stretch and so prevent the collar from choking it.

▶ TOYS ◀

Visit any pet store or supermarket and you will see a vast array of cat toys, such as fluffy or plastic balls.

Cats generally enjoy soft toys that they can grip with their claws. Hard plastic toys are rather frustrating, although balls that roll along provide them with the opportunity to chase, and some cats seem to enjoy the challenge of trying to get a grip on them.

Toys that stimulate through sight or sound are also useful – look for the brightly colored 'wands' that are often used by breeders to get their cat looking animated in front of a judge, and by cat photographers to help them capture an appealing portrait.

Whatever type of toy you buy, make sure it doesn't have any small metal or plastic pieces that could be chewed off and swallowed.

You certainly don't have to spend much money on toys. Small balls of rolled-up newspaper or pieces of cloth attached to a piece of string will serve the purpose. Many cats soon tire of a toy that they deem to be too artificial. A lump of fur or a feather is by far the most interesting and stimulating, although in the paws of an agile cat the latter won't last very long.

Above: *Take care that your cat's toys do not have any small metal or plastic pieces that could be bitten off and swallowed.*

▶ A SCRATCHING POST ◀

Claw-marking – when cats use their claws to scratch objects – is not confined to domestic cats: lions, tigers, leopards, and many other types of cat go through a similar routine.

Claw-marking has two functions. One is territorial, and the claw marks could be described as 'cat graffiti'. The scratches are a visual signal that another cat owns or visits this particular piece of territory. A certain amount of scent, left on the object from the glands on the footpads, reinforces the signal and identifies the individual who left it.

The second function of claw-marking is cosmetic; the scratching action helps to remove dead layers of the protein keratin from the surface of the claws, keeping them sharp and in good working order.

The innate need to claw-mark can get some cats into trouble, especially if they are not provided with a suitable

object, such as a scratching post, on which to carry out this important function.

You can buy a ready-made scratching post, although it is simple to make your own from a soft wood such as pine, and cover it with carpet offcuts, textured cloth or bark. The post must have a heavy base to prevent it from falling over as a result of the cat's vigorous scratching.

Even when a scratching post is available, the best lounge suite may still prove more attractive – you will need patience and your cat will need training (*see pp83–84*). Initially the scratching post should be placed close to the furniture, and the latter protected to discourage the cat and prevent further damage. Because scent is left on the furniture during the scratching action, this needs to be masked by the use of a deodorizing agent or repellent spray. The post can be gradually moved away from the furniture to a mutually acceptable place.

Above: *Teach your cats to use a scratching post as soon as possible – it will be difficult to persuade them to leave the furniture alone after they've had this freedom for a few years.*

CARING FOR YOUR CAT

▶ A CAT DOOR ◀

If your cat is allowed to go outside, a cat door is highly recommended. One possible disadvantage, though, is that neighboring cats might also learn to use it, and pay unexpected and annoying visits. They may even eat your cat's food!

To prevent this problem, it is possible to buy a sophisticated type of cat door with which your cat wears a collar with its own electronic 'pass' system.

▶ A CARRYING BASKET ◀

A carrying basket is not essential, but is very useful, especially when taking a nervous cat to the veterinarian. There are various types, from folding cardboard designs (which cannot be cleaned and have a limited lifespan) to permanent models with plastic trays with wire tops and lids, or fully molded bodies with air holes and front-opening doors.

▶ ARRIVING HOME WITH YOUR NEW CAT ◀

If you have brought home a kitten, in most cases it will just have been taken away from its mother or littermates, and that companionship will need to be replaced. One or more members of the family should act as a surrogate companion for as much time as possible. That means lots of cuddles by responsible people, but only when the kitten wants them. Handle it gently, and restrict the amount of handling that it gets, especially by children. If you have brought home two kittens, then they will be company for each other.

Introduce new experiences gradually, and avoid stressing your kitten or cat with loud or sudden noises. It will usually take several days for a new kitten or cat to adapt to the routines, sights, sounds and smells of your household environment.

Top: *Make sure your cat flap is about 2⅓ in (6cm) above the floor indoors, so the cat is able to simply step through it.*
Above: *A cat carrying basket must be strong, well ventilated, and easy to carry and clean.*

FOOD AND WATER

For the first few days at home you should feed your new cat the same diet it was accustomed to getting from its previous owner. After that, if you wish, you can gradually introduce a new diet over a period of four days, replacing about a quarter of the old diet with the same amount of the new one each day. Make sure that clean, fresh water is always available. This is especially important if your cat is being fed a high proportion of dry food.

SAFETY

When preparing for a kitten's arrival, think about safety in the home, just as you would for a young child.

○ Lock away all household chemicals or poisonous substances. Although kittens are far less inquisitive than puppies and much less likely to ingest poisonous substances, it is best to be on the safe side.

○ Make sure that there are no frayed or bare electrical wires that a kitten could try to chew or play with.

○ Be aware of the risks associated with some common garden plants.

○ Remember that sparks from a fire or cigarette ash can burn eyes or skin.

○ Make sure anyone using lawnmowers, bicycles, skateboards, roller blades, or similar articles is extra vigilant.

○ Check where the kitten is before moving a vehicle.

○ Make sure the kitten cannot get through the fencing around a swimming pool.

Top: *Territory is very important to cats, and windows serve as a good vantage point for a cat to survey its 'property'.*

INFECTIONS YOU COULD CATCH FROM YOUR CAT

Some cat infections, such as the roundworm *Toxocara cati*, ringworm infection, and toxoplasmosis, can be passed on to humans. And if your cat scratches you, you could get cat-scratch fever. (*For more details, see pp112–115.*)

Explain the risks to all family members, and insist on basic hygiene, such as the regular washing of hands and immediate cleansing of any wounds. A doctor should see any deep wounds inflicted by your cat.

HOUSE RULES

As a new member of the family, your kitten or cat must learn where it fits in. Because cats are more independent and solitary than dogs, they don't easily fit into a 'pack' order. Nevertheless, they will learn to obey commands and accept that human members of the family are to be treated as dominant. Teach your cat or kitten some basic house rules, for example, that it may not jump onto the kitchen counter or the dining table, that it may not beg at the table, and that it cannot always have its own way.

Above: *A cat marks its territory by claw-marking or by rubbing its head and face against an object, depositing scent from the sebaceous glands.*

TOILET TRAINING

Cats are naturally clean animals, and if you have provided a litterbox in the correct location, away from food, an adult cat will quickly learn to use it. Kittens need to be taught to use a litterbox though, and you can do this by placing them into it when you think they are about to urinate or defecate. Toiletting occurs most frequently just after waking up and after meals, and if you place a kitten into the litterbox at these times, it will soon learn to use it on cue.

TERRITORY

Your new cat or kitten needs to learn the extent of your territory, come to terms with neighboring cats, and figure out which cat owns what.

Start by keeping your cat shut in your home (even in one room, if necessary) until it feels secure. Then, if you are able, allow it to venture outside. Try to allow it to establish its own territory and make its own peace or friendship with neighboring cats. Some of these may already regard your garden or yard as their own, and strongly object to the presence of your newcomer. You may be able to help your new cat to establish and defend its new territory by discouraging intruders; but in many cases a better and more permanent solution is to let the cats sort out the problem among themselves. There may be lots of noise for a while, but hopefully there will be few, if any, battle scars.

VACCINATIONS

The usual age for a kitten to commence its course of vaccinations against common viral diseases (such as cat flu and snuffles) is between nine and 12 weeks.

Under special circumstances, the first vaccination can be given at six weeks. If you have purchased a pedigree kitten it may already have completed its initial vaccination program, and an adult cat obtained from a rescue center should already have been vaccinated. A separate vaccine is used to protect cats against feline leukemia.

Talk to the staff at your veterinary clinic to find out what vaccines are needed in your area.

Top: *Cats mark their territory by claw-marking furnishings or wallpaper, which can often lead to unhappiness between cat and owner.*

DE-SEXING

Neutered cats of either sex make the best pets. There are already thousands of unwanted kittens needing good homes, so unless you are breeding from pedigree cats, please don't add to their number.

Ask your veterinary clinic about the best age to have your kitten neutered. Most veterinarians recommend that females be spayed between 24–30 weeks old – before they commence their first estrus (that is, 'come into season'). The average age for estrus is about six months, but some individuals of 'precocious' breeds, such as the Siamese, may start 'calling' as early as four and a half months. Some cats don't have their first estrus until they are nine months old, or even older.

Males can be castrated from 16 weeks, but many vets prefer to leave them until they are about six months old. They believe that this allows more time for the development of the urethra, which leads from the bladder through the penis, and thereby reduces the likelihood of the blockage that causes the condition known as feline urological syndrome (FUS). Males should certainly be neutered by nine months, before they have fully developed their male characteristics, learned to roam, and started fighting.

DE-WORMING

Various types of worms can infect kittens and cats. When you get your kitten or cat, it may already have been de-wormed. If not, it may need treatment. Either way, as soon as you get your cat, talk to your vet about what worms are prevalent in your area, what treatments are recommended, and how often you should use them. (*For further information, see pp112-115.*)

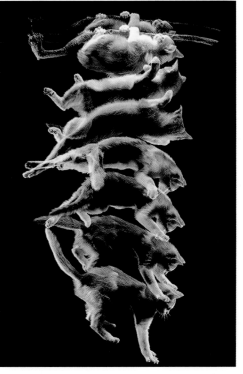

Top: *Although cats are essentially solitary creatures, they do enjoy the company of other cats, especially if they have been brought up together.*
Above: *It is not merely an 'old wives' tale' – cats have a superb sense of balance and usually do land on their feet.*

FLEA CONTROL

Fleas are a common problem and your kitten or cat should have been treated and be free of fleas before you obtain it. However, it will need further, regular treatment against them. Modern treatments are relatively easy to administer. (*For further information, see p111.*)

EXERCISE

Kittens and cats usually exercise themselves, and you will contribute when you become involved in play sessions. If your cat becomes lazy, you may need to encourage it to play.

TRAINING

Basic training for cats involves toilet training and obeying house rules. It is also useful to train your cat to travel in a cage, and to get used to being parted from you. Then, if you need to take it to the vet or to a kennel, it should not be upset or stressed. This type of training is especially useful if your cat is particularly shy or nervous.

First, you must allow the cat to get used to being put into a carrying cage. Initially, leave it in the cage in one of your rooms for a few minutes, then take it out and reward it with food or a cuddle. Extend the period of caging until it is content to remain in the cage for up to an hour.

Next, put it in the cage, carry it outside and place it in a vehicle parked in a quiet spot. Make sure there is adequate ventilation. Leave the cat there for a short time, then bring it back inside. Release it and reward it.

Gradually extend the time you leave it in the vehicle. Finally, if you have a willing relative, friend or neighbor, leave it in the cage with them for short periods. This gets your cat used to being separated from you, and it learns that you will be coming back.

Pet cats can be taught (or sometimes teach themselves) simple tricks such as pulling on a handle to open a door. If you watch advertisements for pet food, videos, or movies, you will be aware that cats can be trained to perform simple tricks. However, this is a specialist area in which you are not likely to become involved. If you do wish to do so, you need to get expert advice.

(*For more information on training and behavior, see pp72–85.*)

Above: *Patience and practice might persuade your Siamese, Burmese, or Russian Blue to walk on a harness.*

TEETHING

Between the ages of 14 weeks and six months your kitten's temporary (milk) teeth will gradually be shed and replaced by permanent teeth. Shedding normally starts with the incisors, followed by the premolar, molar, and then the canine teeth.

Your cat will usually get through this process without you even noticing, and it shouldn't need any special help with its diet. If it does seem to have a problem eating though, provide a moister diet. If this doesn't solve the problem, talk to your vet.

DENTAL HYGIENE

For cats, as with humans, a proper diet that includes plenty of dry or chewable food will help to keep teeth clean and gums healthy. Nevertheless, tartar may begin to accumulate on the teeth, especially as a cat gets older, and they should be checked regularly.

Top: *Take your kitten to the vet for a health check. A runny nose and eyes could indicate a serious problem.*
Right: *Grooming keeps the cat's coat glossy, clean, and healthy, and it also stimulates blood circulation.*

▶ GROOMING ◀

Cats groom themselves to keep their fur clean, and to regulate body temperature. Because of their thick fur, cats' sweat glands are not as effective as those in a human. In hot weather or after strenuous activity, a cat cannot lose enough heat by sweating alone, so it compensates by licking saliva onto its fur; the saliva evaporates, which helps to keep the cat cool. This explains why a cat grooms itself more after spending time in the sun and after exercise such as playing or hunting. Licking the fur also stimulates sebaceous glands in the skin. These secrete an oily fluid that helps to keep the cat's fur waterproof – the fluid also contains a small amount of vitamin D, which the cat then ingests.

Most cats need very little grooming help from their owners. Some are lazy, though, and don't groom themselves enough. If you wish, you can stimulate such a cat to groom by spreading a little butter onto its fur.

Some cats can't groom themselves properly because of their long hair or because of old age. You will need to groom such a cat regularly.

Above: *When grooming your cat, it is important to place it on a non-slip surface, such as a piece of carpet.*

BRUSHING AND COMBING

Get your cat used to being handled and groomed. Establish a daily routine in which the cat is gently placed onto a non-slip surface (a piece of old carpet or something similar) on a table, and rolled over to have its mouth, teeth, eyes, ears, abdomen, and paws examined.

Although it may not need grooming, do it anyway. It will help to train your cat, and you will more quickly detect fleas or flea dirt, and any hair or skin problems. Try to make each session pleasant for the cat, and praise and reward it for good behavior. Your basic grooming equipment should include a cat brush, comb, grooming glove (mitt), sponge, cotton balls, cat towel, blunt-ended surgical scissors, and (if you wish) nail clippers.

There are various types of cat combs. Some have wide teeth, and can be used on long, fine coats. Some have teeth of varying lengths, and others have only fine teeth (flea combs). There is also a special type of comb with wire projections for use on a thick undercoat to remove tangled hair, as well as a 'slicker' brush for use on the tail, especially before a show.

When grooming a longhaired cat, pay special attention to the feathering on the legs and the tail. Matted fur may occur in areas that the cat cannot easily reach to groom, such as on the inside of the elbows and along the abdomen close to the thighs. Also check the paws, nails, and paw pads. In longhaired cats, hair may grow beyond the level of the pads. If so, trim it away using a pair of blunt-ended, curved surgical scissors. Also check under the tail, wipe away any debris and cut away any excess hair.

Use a damp cotton wool ball to wipe away 'sleep' from your cat's eyes.

BATHING

If you carry out regular grooming, it will seldom be necessary to bath your cat – unless it becomes particularly dirty or smelly, or just before a cat show.

Always give your cat a thorough brush before bathing it. Use lukewarm water, which is more comfortable, and a shampoo made for cats. Don't let shampoo get into any body opening. Rinse thoroughly, paying special attention to the areas between the forelegs and hind legs.

A cat can easily become chilled when wet, so make sure you dry it well afterwards, using its own special towel. If you prefer to use a hair dryer, run your fingers through the cat's hair as it is being dried to make sure that the air stream is not too hot.

Above: *Some cats do tolerate being bathed, especially if introduced to the procedure gently and while they are still kittens. Take care to dry your cat thoroughly afterwards, as cats easily become chilled.*

NAILS

A cat's nails, like those of humans, are continually growing. The action of claw-marking is usually enough to keep them worn down and in good shape, but in some cases the nails will need cutting with nail clippers. You may be able to do this yourself, or you may find it easier to ask someone at your local veterinary clinic or a cat groomer to do it for you.

CAT GROOMERS AND GROOMING PARLORS

Many pedigree cat breeds, especially those with long coats, require considerable grooming. If you know what to do and you have the time, you can do this yourself. If not, you can get an expert to do it for you.

If you would like to learn to groom your cat, ask at your nearest grooming parlor or vet for details of grooming schools, or courses being offered, in your area.

Top and above left: *When a cat scratches a tree, an old claw sheath may come off and be left in the bark.*
Above right: *A longhaired cat needs daily grooming – up to 20 minutes at a time.*

▶ TRAVELING WITH YOUR CAT ◀

Whenever you take your cat away from home, make sure it is wearing a suitable elasticated collar that bears a tag with your name and telephone number, or an electronic identichip (a relatively cheap, effective, and increasingly common hi-tech method of keeping track of your pet).

IN YOUR CAR

If possible, train your cat from kittenhood to get used to traveling. Early training will help eliminate any fear or agitation, and reduce the likelihood of motion sickness.

Don't let your cat have complete freedom inside a vehicle. It can distract the driver and lead to an accident, which also puts the cat at risk of injury. For its own safety the cat should be in a plastic or metal traveling cage, which should be fastened by a seat belt to reduce the chance of injury in the event of an accident.

If your cat is likely to travel in your car quite often, train it to do so as soon as you can. Your cat's travel cage eventually becomes an extension of its home territory, and it will feel comfortable inside and readily occupy it. Travel cages are commonly used by people who show their cats, and are an ideal way of providing a safe, secure, 'personal space' for your feline companion. Once your cat is accustomed to it, the cage can accompany it wherever it goes, providing it with a 'home away from home'.

If you have to leave your cat in the car, make sure that the vehicle is parked in the shade and has adequate ventilation. In the sun, the temperature inside a closed car can quickly exceed 100°, and heatstroke can set in very rapidly. Do not assume that a car parked in the shade will remain so: as the sun moves around, a shady area may become fully exposed. Special screens can be fixed to open windows to provide car security as well as ventilation.

Top: *Many cats learn to travel well if they start as kittens. If your journey is to last for longer than an hour, schedule regular breaks to allow your cat to eat, drink and use its litterbox.*

ON VACATION

Make sure that your cat's vaccinations are up to date, because the incidence of infectious disease in the area of your destination may be greater than in your home neighborhood. Different sorts of external parasites, such as ticks, may also be present, so groom your cat thoroughly every day and check its skin for their presence.

If you are staying in one place, make a note of the nearest veterinary clinic.

IN A BUS, TRAIN OR PLANE

If you are taking some form of commercial transport, your cat may be required to travel separately in a cage. This can be a frightening experience for a cat that has not been cage-trained, so anticipate the event and train your cat to feel safe in its own crate, with its own familiar toys and bedding. Don't feed your cat within six hours of the start of the journey. If you think it may suffer from motion sickness, ask your vet for advice.

TRAVELING BETWEEN COUNTRIES

Travel between countries usually involves travel documentation for your cat as well as yourself. Regulations vary, so make sure you know what they are for the particular country you are visiting. You will probably need a veterinary certificate stating that your cat is fit to travel and

Above: *Train your cat to feel safe in its own carrier, with its familiar toys and bedding.*

CARING FOR YOUR CAT

is free from any infectious or contagious diseases. You will also require an up-to-date rabies vaccination certificate. Many countries require these documents to be in their own language.

There are many countries where rabies does not exist. These include the United Kingdom and certain other European countries. Some islands, such as Hawaii, Australia and New Zealand, are also rabies-free. Some countries require a cat to be quarantined upon entry, others will allow entry providing that certain conditions, such as microchip identification and blood testing, are met (*see the PETS Travel Scheme, below*).

When making plans for international travel, contact the consulate or embassy of the country concerned. Information may also be available on the Internet.

If traveling abroad requires you and your cat to be separated, carry out the training procedures recommended for commercial travel on a bus, train or plane (*see above*).

THE EUROPEAN PETS TRAVEL SCHEME

A pilot scheme for the issue of pet passports was introduced in Britain in late February 2000. Under this scheme, cats and dogs are allowed to travel from the British Isles to specified countries in western Europe and return home without having to endure six months of quarantine upon their return. Owners must use designated carriers and ports of entry, and cannot import a pet under the PETS Travel Scheme from a private boat or plane.

Cats and dogs resident in certain European countries that are taking part in the scheme are also allowed to enter the British Isles. At the time of writing participating countries were Andorra, Australia (Guide dogs and Hearing dogs only), Austria, Belgium, Denmark, Finland, France, Germany, Greece, Iceland, Italy, Liechtenstein, Luxembourg, Monaco, Netherlands, New Zealand (Guide dogs and Hearing dogs only), Norway, Portugal, San Marino, Spain, Sweden and Switzerland.

RESIDENT CATS IN THE BRITISH ISLES

To qualify for a passport, a cat resident in the British Isles must have an identification microchip inserted under the skin. When the cat is at least three months old, an approved veterinarian must then vaccinate it against rabies. Some time after the last vaccine injection (30 days is the ideal period), a blood sample is taken by the veterinarian and sent to one of the government-approved laboratories. Only once the sample has passed the test can a health certificate or passport be issued and stamped by the veterinarian.

Between 24 and 48 hours before returning to Britain, the cat must be treated against a particular tapeworm and ticks, and a veterinarian approved by the relevant government must issue a health certificate.

Once a cat has been vaccinated against rabies, booster vaccinations are required every year to keep it valid.

RESIDENT CATS IN DESIGNATED EUROPEAN COUNTRIES

Animals resident in specified countries in Europe can also qualify to enter Britain if their owners follow the same rules. However, their owners must wait for six months from the time a successful blood test sample was taken.

RESIDENT CATS IN THE UNITED STATES AND CANADA

Because rabies is endemic in North America, the original PETS Travel Scheme does not apply to cats entering from the United States or Canada. At the time of writing, these cats must still endure a six month period of quarantine in Britain before being granted entrance. However, it is expected that the situation will be reviewed once the success of the initial scheme has been assessed.

Resident cats in rabies-free islands

If the PETS travel scheme proves successful, it will be extended gradually. Providing that the relevant veterinary authorities and the airline carriers agree, cats and dogs may be allowed to travel between Britain and designated islands that are rabies-free.

BOARDING CATTERIES

Most cats adjust very quickly to going to a boarding cattery. The standard of catteries varies and usually (but not always) you get what you pay for; the more expensive the service, the better the quality of comfort and care you should expect. A reputable cattery will allow you to inspect its facilities beforehand. If you do so, observe how the resident cats are behaving and talk to the staff about feeding, grooming, and exercise routines.

The staff at your local veterinary clinic may be able to recommend a suitable cattery, and will advise on vaccination procedures. Reputable catteries require their boarders to have up-to-date vaccination certificates against common infectious diseases.

CAT-SITTERS

If you don't like the idea of boarding your cat, you may choose to employ a cat-sitter or house minder to provide live-in care of your home and your cat while you're away. Your local veterinarian should be able to give you contact details of people in your area willing to provide this service.

Above: *Traveling internationally with your cat requires an enormous amount of organization, not least having to make sure that you have the correct, legally specified container for your animal.*

Above: *Before you book your cat into a boarding cattery, visit the premises to check whether they are clean and spacious.*

4. NUTRITION

▶ A BALANCED DIET ◀

Like all animals, the domestic cat needs a diet that is properly balanced and contains all the essential nutrients in the correct quantities. These nutrients are water, protein, fat, carbohydrates, minerals, and vitamins.

The wild members of the cat family (*Felidae*) such as the lion, tiger, cheetah, and European wild cat, are carnivores. Between them they hunt and kill a wide variety of other animals, ranging in size from small lizards and birds to large antelopes. They don't just eat the meat or muscle, but consume all – or almost all – of their prey, including the skin, hair or feathers, and the internal organs such as liver, kidneys, and intestines. Their diet therefore contains a substantial amount of animal protein, and this supplies them with all the other essential nutrients that they require.

To remain healthy, domestic cats also require a diet containing animal protein. This is because they need a particular amino acid (one of the building blocks of protein) called taurine, which helps to prevent heart and eye diseases. Taurine is plentiful in animal protein, but only present in small amounts in plant protein.

While dogs are able to manufacture the amino acid taurine within their body, cats can only manufacture a little, and this is not enough to meet their needs. Plant protein does not supply enough to make up the shortfall. Therefore, although a pet dog could remain healthy if fed a properly balanced vegetarian diet, a cat cannot.

For this reason, cats are known as obligatory carnivores; they must eat some animal protein on a daily basis in order to survive.

▶ WATER ◀

Water is the most important element in a cat's diet. Whereas most animals can survive after losing up to half of their protein and stored fat, even a 10 per cent loss of total body water in a cat will cause serious illness, and a 15 per cent loss will result in death.

Animals can ingest water in three ways. They drink it, eat food containing it, and their body manufactures some as a by-product of the chemical processes involved in converting proteins, fats, and carbohydrates into energy.

The daily amount of water required by a cat is determined by the cat's energy output. A sedentary cat needs a daily intake of about 2 tablespoons of water for each pound of body weight, while an active cat needs just under 3 tablespoons of water per pound of body weight.

Opposite: *Even well-fed cats hunt occasionally. A balanced diet incorporates all the nutrients a cat would get from its natural prey.*

▶ PROTEIN ◀

Protein is found in animals (animal protein) and in plants (plant protein). There are many different types of protein, each of which contains a particular combination of amino acids, the substances that provide the materials needed for the growth and repair of all body tissues.

Proteins vary in their digestibility. The most digestible for cats are those contained in foods derived from animal sources, such as meat, eggs, and cheese. The least digestible for cats are those contained in foods derived from plants, such as grains and vegetables. Most domestic cats consume a diet containing a significant amount of animal protein. They do eat some plant material, either in the stomach and intestines of prey that they catch, or by voluntarily eating specific plants such as grass. But overall, plant protein is a comparatively unimportant part of the domestic cat's diet.

When a cat eats grass it is probably doing so to consume fiber, an aid to digestion. Quite often a cat will vomit soon afterwards, bringing up a bolus of grass mixed with mucus, so eating grass may be a useful method of getting rid of excess mucus from the cat's stomach.

▶ FATS ◀

Fats and oils contain substances called fatty acids, some of which play an important role in helping to maintain certain internal body functions and healthy skin. They also act as carriers for the fat-soluble vitamins (A, D, E, and K). Fats are a concentrated form of energy (for a given weight, fat provides more than twice as many kilocalories as carbohydrates or protein).

If the diet that a cat consumes contains more energy than the cat needs, the excess is converted into fat and stored in various parts of the body such as under the skin and around the intestines. This fat acts as a fuel store that can be drawn upon in times of need.

Opposite: *Most cats are disciplined eaters and will eat little, often. Some cats, however, will eat all the food in their bowls, no matter how much there is.*

NUTRITION

▶ CARBOHYDRATES ◀

Carbohydrates occur in plants and include sugars, starch, and cellulose. There are various types of sugars, including sucrose and glucose. These are two of the simplest sugars and therefore more easily digested. Cow's milk contains the milk sugar lactose, but many adult cats are unable to digest lactose properly. For this reason specially formulated lactose-reduced or lactose-free milk is available for cats from pet food stores and supermarkets. For cats, one of the most useful sources of dietary carbohydrate is rice.

▶ MINERALS ◀

Like other animals, the cat needs to consume many different minerals to ensure that its body processes function normally. Some are required in comparatively large amounts, while others, known as trace elements, are only required in very small quantities. Two of the most important minerals for felines are calcium and phosphorus, which are involved in the formation and growth of bones and teeth. Minerals also play an important role in the growth and repair of body tissues such as muscles, ligaments, skin, and hair. They are also required in the formation of red and white blood cells, and in various digestive processes.

▶ VITAMINS ◀

Certain vitamins are essential for the proper working of body processes. Four of them, vitamins A, D, E, and K, are soluble in fat, so fats and oils are essential dietary elements. Vitamins A and D play a particularly important role in bone growth. Vitamin E plays an important role in normal muscle function, vision, and reproductive processes. Vitamins of the B-group, and vitamin C, are soluble in water. The B-group vitamins have a variety of functions associated with the metabolism of amino acids, fats, or carbohydrates. Vitamin C is involved in wound healing, preventing hemorrhages from small blood vessels (capillaries), and maintaining healthy skin. As in humans, vitamin C is important in the prevention of scurvy. Cats, like dogs, have the ability to manufacture this vitamin within their bodies and therefore, unlike humans, don't need a source of vitamin C in their diet.

▶ FIBER ◀

Derived from plant materials (often ingested along with prey), fiber does not provide a cat with any nutrients, but it does play a very important role in digestion. It acts as a bulking agent, absorbs any toxic by-products of the digestive processes, and increases the rate of passage of food through the gut.

► ENERGY ◄

Energy is measured in kilojoules. It is not classified as a nutrient, but is the 'fuel' that a cat derives from the protein, fat and carbohydrates that it eats. Cats require sufficient kilojoules to fulfil their basic energy needs, and this amount varies according to their size and circumstances. Adult cats do not have such a great range of sizes and weights as adult dogs. There are variations between breeds and individuals, but most adult domestic cats weigh between 5.5 lb (2.5kg) and 10 lb (5.5kg). Sedentary house cats need less energy than active cats that spend a lot of time outdoors. Energy use also varies according to environmental temperature, being greater in very cold temperatures or in hot, tropical climates. Comparatively more energy is required per pound of body weight by a queen in late pregnancy and during lactation, by a kitten when growing, and by any cat during illness, recuperation or stress.

Given the opportunity to self-feed (for example, self-feeding on dry pet food and/or freedom to hunt), some cats will feed little and often, exercise themselves, and remain within a satisfactory weight range. Others will eat everything on offer, and if their owner does not monitor their energy intake, can quickly become obese.

It is not unusual for domestic cats to put on weight in fall and winter and lose it again in the summer. This probably reflects the situation in the wild, where many animals lay down a store of fat prior to winter when food becomes scarce. When cats put on excessive weight and keep it on, it is usually the result of overeating or lack of exercise, or a combination of both. In this case their energy intake should be strictly monitored, because overweight cats, just like overweight humans, are more likely to have health problems.

A GUIDE TO ENERGY REQUIREMENTS FOR CATS	
ACTIVITY	APPROXIMATE DAILY ENERGY NEED Kilojoules per pound
Sedentary	30–32
Active	38-40
Gestation (last 3 weeks)	41–45
Lactation	63–77 (depending on the number of kittens in the litter)
Growth (weaning to 6 months)	59
Growth (6–12 months)	45

► COMMERCIAL OR HOME-COOKED FOOD? ◄

Fast foods are as readily available for cats as they are for humans. Take a walk around any supermarket and you will see a vast array of canned, packaged, and frozen options. There are foods for kittens, adult cats, and mature cats. Many pet stores and veterinary clinics sell various 'professional formulas', some for ordinary maintenance of a normal cat, and others for specific health problems.

When deciding whether to feed your cat a commercial diet or to cook meals yourself, there are various factors to consider. Many commercial diets are complete and balanced, which means that they will provide all the nutrients your cat needs. There is less certainty, though, that a homemade diet will be properly balanced.

You may also need to consider the costs and convenience. Many commercial diets are more expensive than home-cooked ones, but home-cooked diets involve time, careful planning, preparation, and storage. For that reason most cat owners find it convenient to feed their cats one of the reputable commercial diets and, if they wish, offer homemade 'treats' from time to time. Pregnant queens, kittens, young growing cats, and geriatric cats all have special dietary needs, so it is best to feed them a commercial diet specially formulated for their situation. Offer the occasional homemade meal to give your cat a break in routine.

▶ COMMERCIAL DIETS ◀

Many commercial diets are formulated to provide all your cat's nutritional requirements. They are formulated by nutritional scientists and veterinarians and have been tried and tested in controlled feeding trials to meet approved international standards.

There is a bewildering choice of commercial cat food. There are 'mainstream' foods, comparatively cheap, for the 'average' cat. There are 'premium' foods, often packaged in small quantities, that appeal to the human eye (and sometimes, but not always, to the cat's taste buds) and are more expensive. Your cat can have a choice of lamb, beef, chicken, tuna, sardines, or ocean fish, to name but a few. Some foods contain combinations, such as beef and chicken. The nutritional profile of all these foods is very similar; it is just the contents that vary.

Commercial cat diets can be grouped according to their moisture content.

O Canned or moist foods. These have a moisture content of around 78 per cent (roughly the same as fresh meat) and do not need preservatives because cooking destroys all bacteria and the canning prevents any further contamination. Because they contain no preservatives, if they are not used immediately after opening they require refrigeration.

O Semi-moist foods. These have a moisture content of around 30 per cent and normally contain preservatives. Some do not require refrigeration. They are commonly fed as 'treats'.

O Dry foods (complete diets). These have a moisture content of around 10 per cent, normally contain preservatives, and do not require refrigeration. They are hygienic, easy to store, and available for cats of all ages.

It is impossible to compare the relative nutritional value and price of all available products.

To find out if a commercial food is fully balanced, check the label. There should be some statement to the effect of: 'complete and balanced', and some labels bear a distinguishing mark that denotes that they have been tested and approved. Some formulas contain textured vegetable protein (TVP) as well as animal protein, because TVP is cheaper.

You will probably base your choice on a product's price, how readily your cat will eat it, and its labeled food content. The label usually lists the main food ingredients, and an analysis of certain nutrients such as protein, fat, and salt. Many manufacturers list the caloric value of the food, which can help you to decide how much to feed. Additionally, some indicate the amount that should be fed relative to body weight, stage of growth, and activity level.

FOODS FROM THE VETERINARY CLINIC AND PET STORES

There are a number of international companies that manufacture cat foods known as 'professional formulas'.

Available only from selected pet stores and from most veterinary clinics, these differ from supermarket pet foods in that their constituents are guaranteed. What this means is that a cat food made of chicken, for example, will always contain a specified amount of chicken, no matter how high the cost of poultry at the time of production. These products do not contain the TVP that is found in some supermarket products.

Other foods sold only through veterinary clinics are therapeutic diets formulated to assist in the management of certain health problems, such as

Above: *Like their human 'owners', cats love to eat, but unlike humans they are able to lose up to 40 per cent of their body weight without losing their lives.*

allergies, gastro-intestinal disorders, kidney and bladder disorders, liver disease, and obesity. Special diets are available for pregnant and lactating queens, to assist cats recovering after surgery or trauma, or for those undergoing treatment for conditions such as anemia or cancer. If you want more information about any of these diets, you should talk to your local veterinarian.

▶ HOME-COOKED DIETS ◀

If you want to prepare some or all of your cat's meals yourself, and can ensure that it receives a properly balanced diet containing adequate amounts of animal protein, then by all means do so. If your cat has access to the outdoors, and to natural prey such as mice and lizards, then the chances are that the food it obtains outside will make up for any small deficiency in nutrients that might occur in your home-made diet. If it relies entirely on the food you provide, you must be absolutely sure that the diet you offer is correctly balanced.

The animal protein for a home-cooked diet is usually derived from red meat, liver, kidney, heart, chicken, fish, and (to a much lesser extent) milk. Remember that cooking food destroys some vitamins, and overcooking greatly reduces its nutritional value, so you need to supplement cooked food with the correct amounts and proportions of vitamins, just as reputable pet food manufacturers do. Pet food supplements usually contain calcium carbonate or bonemeal (to create the right balance of calcium and phosphorus, which is crucial), iodine, and vitamins A and D. You can purchase properly formulated supplements and various herbal preparations from a good pet store or from some veterinary clinics.

Before basing your cat's diet on home-cooked foods and/or using any form of supplement, though, talk to your vet. Excessive supplementation with vitamins and minerals can cause serious health problems.

Supplementation of a home-cooked or commercial diet may sometimes be necessary for certain health conditions, such as stress, illness or post-operative recovery. In such cases you should always ask your veterinarian for advice, and he or she may recommend a change to one of the specially formulated therapeutic diets.

Top left and right: *Canned commercial diets contain balanced nutrients, but do not help maintain healthy teeth and gums. Feeding dry food as well helps to overcome this problem.*

INGREDIENTS FOR HOME-COOKED MEALS

Even if you decide to make commercial cat foods the basis of your cat's diet, you may still find some of the information in this section useful.

MEAT AND MEAT BY-PRODUCTS

All forms of red or white meat provide protein, B-group vitamins, fat, and energy, but the relative amounts depend on the type and cut of meat.

Chicken is considered to be more digestible than red meat. Some types of meat and offal are seriously deficient in calcium and slightly deficient in phosphorus. In other meats, the proportion of phosphorus to calcium may be

Top: *Cats enjoy eating prepared liver, although it is unwise to feed it to cats more than once a week. Large amounts of liver can give the cat too much vitamin A, which causes skeletal problems.*

excessive. This can range, for instance, from about 10:1 for rabbit and ox heart to 30:1 for veal and 360:1 for fresh liver. Meat is also deficient in vitamins A and D and iodine, copper, iron, magnesium and sodium. Therefore, meat should be supplemented, particularly with calcium, if it is to form a balanced diet. Meat is most nutritious if fed raw, because cooking destroys much of its vitamin B content.

Liver is a valuable food rich in protein, fat, fat-soluble vitamins (A, D, and E) and the B vitamins. Cooking reduces the liver's vitamin A content, but this is not a problem because too much vitamin A can lead to abnormal bone growth. As a general guide, do not let liver form more than 10 per cent of the cat's diet.

FISH

There are two main types of fish. White fish has a nutrient composition similar to lean meat, contains less than two per cent fat, and is deficient in the fat-soluble vitamins (A, D, E, and K).

Fatty and oily fish (such as tuna) contain high levels of vitamins A and D and high levels of unsaturated fatty acids. Feeding your cat too much may cause a painful inflammation of fat deposits under the skin (steatitis).

Both white and oily types of fish contain high-quality protein and iodine. However, they are unfortunately deficient in calcium, phosphorus, copper, iron, magnesium, and sodium.

Take care not to feed your cat too much raw (filleted) fish, as it contains thiaminase, an enzyme that destroys thiamine, one of the important B vitamins. Thiaminase is inactivated by heat, so it is best to cook fish before feeding it to your cat. Fish bones can cause problems if they get caught in a cat's teeth or stuck in its throat, so if you are feeding whole (unfilleted) fish, make sure that the bones have been softened by boiling, stewing, or pressure cooking (this rather old-fashioned style of cooking is the ideal way to prepare fish bones for both cats and dogs). Whole fish fed in this way is nutritionally better than meat.

RELATIVE NUTRITIONAL VALUES OF MEAT			
Food	Protein (average %)	Fat (average %)	Energy (calories /3.5 oz [100g])
Beef (medium fat)	20	15	220
Chicken (meat)	20	4.5	120
Chicken (necks)	13.2	18	230
Chicken (skin)	16	17	223
Lamb	15	22	265
Liver (ox)	20	3.8	140
Kidney (ox)	15	6.7	130
Heart (ox)	17	3.6	108

Eggs

Eggs contain iron, protein, most vitamins (except for vitamin C), fats, and carbohydrates. Whole eggs contain about 13 per cent protein, 11.5 per cent fat, and provide about 160 kilojoules in every 3.5oz (100g). They are a well-balanced food and a useful source of animal protein and essential nutrients, particularly if fed raw. However, too much raw egg may be harmful, as egg white contains a substance called avidin that can reduce the availability of the B vitamin biotin, essential for many body processes, including healthy skin and hair, and proper muscle function. As a guide, feed no more than one raw egg per week to an adult cat. Cooking eggs by hard-boiling, poaching, or frying reduces the avidin but also reduces their nutritional value, unfortunately. If you feed your cat the egg yolk only, you may increase the number of eggs to two or three per week. Remember that egg yolk on its own has a comparatively high fat content (about 31 per cent) and too much of this could cause obesity.

Milk, cheese and yoghurt

Dairy produce is high in protein, fat, carbohydrates, calcium, phosphorus, vitamin A, and the B vitamins. Whole milk is a useful source of calcium for kittens, and most cats like to drink it. You can serve it warmed, at room temperature, or straight from the fridge – however your cat prefers. Whole milk contains milk sugar (lactose) though, and as kittens mature, their ability to digest it decreases. Cats given large quantities of milk to drink may develop diarrhea. Some adult cats are lactose intolerant, and if fed milk will develop allergic, dry, itchy skin. For this reason, low-lactose cat milk is manufactured and available in supermarkets.

Cream contains most of the milk fat and is a high source of energy, but if fed to excess it could result in obesity.

Cheese is a useful source of animal protein, and some cats like it. It does not contain lactose, so it can be fed in small chunks to cats that are known to have lactose intolerance. Pasteurized yoghurt also does not contain lactose, but not all cats will consume it.

Fats and Oils

A fat deficiency in the diet produces itchy skin that may become dry and flaky.

Fat is almost 100 per cent digestible and adds palatability to food. Vegetable oils and fish fats are nutritionally better than animal fats. Safflower oil and corn oil are excellent sources of fatty acids – but safflower is the best of these two. If your cat's diet is not already balanced, you can feed it very small amounts of cod liver oil (about a quarter of a teaspoon three times per week). Be very careful with such supplementation however, and before doing so talk to your veterinarian. Cod liver oil contains excessive amounts of unsaturated fatty acids and these may cause steatitis.

Vegetables

Most greens are rich in vitamin C, and vegetables are a good source of B-group vitamins. Cats can synthesize vitamin C in their bodies and don't require a dietary source. Some cats will eat greens and vegetables if part of a stew with meat or fish. Remember that overcooking reduces their nutritional value.

Grains

Grains provide carbohydrates and some proteins, minerals and vitamins. They are generally deficient in fat, essential fatty acids, and the fat-soluble vitamins A, D and E.

Wheatgerm contains thiamine and vitamin E. Wheat, oats, and barley have a higher protein content and less fat than corn and rice. Rice is palatable to cats and is used as an ingredient in a number of commercial cat foods.

Yeast is rich in the B vitamins and some minerals, and yeast preparations may be beneficial to older cats – they are safe even if used to excess. Despite anecdotal evidence, dietary supplementation with yeast does not prevent fleas.

Fiber

Your cat's normal diet should contain about five per cent fiber (measured on a dry basis) derived from vegetable matter. Fiber-rich diets (containing about 10–15 per cent fiber) may be used to help reduce obesity, and can also be used as a dietary aid in diabetic cats, as fiber slows the absorption of glucose (the end-product of carbohydrate digestion) following a meal.

Bones

Bones and bonemeal contain 30 per cent calcium and 15 per cent phosphorus, magnesium and proteins. They are deficient in fat, essential fatty acids and vitamins. Too many bones can cause constipation, so ask your vet about quantities.

It is also useful to check with your vet before feeding your cat chicken bones. Mature chicken bones should be avoided because they are liable to splinter, although they can be softened by pressure cooking. Fish bones can get stuck in a cat's mouth or throat and should also be softened by cooking.

Water

Make sure that clean, fresh water is always available. A cat's normal daily requirement (from feeding and drinking) is about one tablespoon per pound of body weight. Water intake will vary according to the environmental temperature and your cat's diet, increasing in proportion to the amount of dry food it consumes. It also increases if your cat is suffering from an ailment such as diarrhea, diabetes, or kidney disease.

FEEDING

Select a feeding area in a cool place where your cat can eat without being disturbed. Use bowls made of easy to clean materials, and wash them after each use.

Cats are known as fussy eaters, but with good reason. A cat will eat only the freshest food it can find, turning up its nose at the smell of anything old or stale. This is because cats are stimulated to eat not only by hunger, but by scent, too. As a rule, they prefer their food warm or at room temperature because it has a better aroma. Some will eat cold, unused canned food that has been refrigerated immediately after use, but others will not.

Because canned (moist) cat food does not contain preservatives, remove any that is uneaten within an hour or so. If flies are a problem, remove uneaten food immediately. Semi-moist food can be left in a bowl for several hours.

If your cat does not overeat, dry foods can be left out all day. If you wish to do this, purchase a self-feeder that keeps the food (and its aroma) enclosed and allows the cat free access.

FEEDING YOUR KITTEN

A queen's milk is rich in protein and fat, and during the first few weeks after weaning, a kitten's diet needs to reflect this. A growing kitten requires up to three times more energy per pound of body weight than an adult and, because it has limited stomach capacity, must be fed several times a day.

There are many commercial brands of food specially formulated for kittens, both grain-based and meat-based. You can also feed milk, although many vets advise against cow's milk, which may cause diarrhea because of its lactose content. A specially formulated cat milk may be better.

As a general guide, a kitten of 8–12 weeks should get at least four meals a day. You need to decide whether you are going to feed it a home-cooked or commercial diet – and stick to it. Mixing can lead to imbalances.

From three to six months, feed the kitten at least three meals a day, and introduce the regime suggested below for adult cats.

Top: *Though there is a wide variety of cat food available, some cats will develop a taste for a particular brand.*

FEEDING YOUR ADULT CAT

Unlike dogs, which are competitive pack animals and will happily wolf down as much food as their stomachs can hold, cats are solitary hunters and don't usually eat a large amount at a time. Given the option, they would prefer to eat their daily ration in several small meals throughout the day.

Most owners find it convenient to feed their cats a mixture of moist and dry foods. Dry foods can be left out for a cat to self-feed throughout the day, and moist foods can be fed in controlled amounts two or three times a day. Late-night feeding can cause problems if your cat is confined to the house during the night, because most cats need to urinate and defecate within an hour or two of feeding.

If you are feeding more than one cat, you may need to feed them separately and some distance apart. This will prevent a dominant cat from eating the other's food. It also makes it possible for you to monitor their individual food intake.

HOW MUCH TO FEED

Most cats tend to eat only enough to satisfy their energy needs. The amount of energy your cat uses will depend not only on its activity, but also on its metabolic rate (the speed at which it burns up the energy in the food). Every cat is an individual, and there can be as much as 20 per cent variation between two similar cats.

Your cat should be fed enough food to satisfy its energy needs, but no more – otherwise it will put on excess weight. Excess energy is stored as fat, deposited under the skin and under the abdomen (causing an appearance referred to as an 'apron'). Some commercial diets are particularly palatable, and stimulate a cat to overeat. If you feed a commercial diet, ascertain its energy content from the label and feed your cat accordingly. If you feed a home-made diet, it may be more difficult to determine exactly how much to feed, and you will need to monitor your cat's health closely.

The most important criteria for judging if you are feeding the correct quantity and balance are the health and appearance of your cat. If it is in good condition, looks alert and active with healthy skin and coat, and maintaining its proper weight, it is almost certainly getting an adequate diet. If it has flaky skin, is shedding its coat excessively, is over- or underweight, appears dull or listless, is excessively hungry or often disinterested in food, you should talk to your vet.

Remember that if you give your cat treats between meals, these contain calories and you must must take this into account when considering your cat's overall diet and calculating its total energy intake.

▶ NUTRITIONAL PROBLEMS ◀

Nutritional problems are unlikely in a cat fed a commercial diet, but may arise if a cat is:

○ receiving the wrong diet
○ eating, but a disease is reducing its ability to absorb or use food
○ not eating for a variety of reasons.

Underfeeding results in lack of energy, weight loss (the body first burns up fat reserves, and then the protein in the muscles), and finally starvation. It could also result in a deficiency of essential nutrients.

Overfeeding causes obesity and perhaps even toxicity caused by a nutrient excess (such as vitamin A).

5. UNDERSTANDING YOUR CAT

▸ THE FELINE SOCIAL SYSTEM ◂

The social system of cats living in a wild state varies in relation to their ecological circumstances – food availability is the major influencing factor. Groups may be formed when the availability and dispersion of food allows two or more individuals to live in close proximity. Most of these groups consist of females, usually related, together with their offspring and immature males.

Females often nurse each other's kittens and bring back prey for them all. Mature males are not part of the 'family' group, forming only loose, temporary liaisons with it for breeding purposes. They are not involved with the rearing of kittens.

Where food is scattered, cats live a more solitary existence. Defended areas contain the denning site and, possibly, a major food source. Territories are formed and demarcated with scent and visual signals, such as scratch marks (claw-marking) and uncovered feces. A cat entering the territory of another risks attack, although home ranges (areas in which hunting is done) may overlap. However, where this occurs, the cats sharing the home range rarely meet. They seem to have some sort of 'time-share' arrangement, which ensures that they hunt in different areas at different times.

Above: *Cats enjoy high places, which is why they favor windows as entry and exit points.*
Opposite: *Pets that grow up together can become good friends.*

▶ THE CAT-HUMAN RELATIONSHIP ◀

Cats are flexible in their dependence on humans, because most cats are capable of surviving in a wild environment. In suburban areas it is difficult to find enough prey to support a totally feral existence, so a liaison with humans is necessary and beneficial. The relationship between cats and humans is one of mutual gain, or symbiosis. Cats gain shelter, a food supply, and health care. We get rodent control and companionship.

Unlike dogs, cats do not necessarily regard humans as part of their own social group. The social order of a group of cats in a household tends to involve only the cats. This does vary, though: cats raised in close contact with humans, and who have no other cats in the household, do regard humans as part of their social group, and may show behavior such as status-related aggression toward them (*see p72*). Some breeds, such as Siamese and Burmese, have been selectively bred for friendliness toward humans and are often very attached to and psychologically dependent on their owners. On the whole, most cats maintain a relatively independent existence and seek human companionship on their own terms.

Above: *It is essential to teach children to hold a cat correctly, so that its weight is supported. An uncomfortable cat will kick and bite in an attempt to free itself.*

▶ A KITTEN'S SOCIAL DEVELOPMENT ◀

Kittens are born blind and deaf. Their eyes open at two weeks and they begin to play at three. At this stage they hear well and have a good sense of smell, and the gape response is shown (*see below*). Vision develops slowly, over a period of 10 weeks.

Play increases in intensity from four to 11 weeks, and then declines. By eight weeks the kittens are capable of killing and eating small prey. It is important that kittens socialize with humans and other cats during the two- to seven-week period, otherwise they will be fearful of human contact and have difficulty integrating with other animals in a household. If hand-reared and isolated from other cats or kittens, they may never relate normally to other cats.

▶ THE CAT'S SENSE OF SMELL ◀

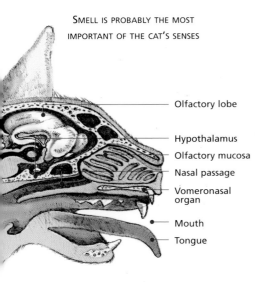

SMELL IS PROBABLY THE MOST IMPORTANT OF THE CAT'S SENSES

- Olfactory lobe
- Hypothalamus
- Olfactory mucosa
- Nasal passage
- Vomeronasal organ
- Mouth
- Tongue

Cats have a keen sense of smell and have a special structure (the vomeronasal organ) that helps them detect scents. This organ consists of two blind-ending tubes that run between the oral and nasal cavities. Substances taken into the mouth are dissolved in fluid contained in the fine tubes, then sensory information is conveyed to the olfactory organs.

When cats are investigating a smell using this organ, they hold their mouths open in a sort of gaping grimace.

Scent is an important means of communication. It is used to define territory via sprayed urine, from scent deposited from facial glands during rubbing, or glands in the feet during scratching. Scent is also deposited onto feces from the anal glands. It is thought that scent conveys information about identity, social

Above: *Cats are able to detect tiny particles of scent, which tell them about the social and reproductive status of other cats. They do this by means of the 'gape' response (also known as 'flehming') – this lip-curling expression delivers the chemicals of the scent to the sensitive vomeronasal organ.*

Top: *Kittens are born blind and deaf and are relatively helpless before two weeks of age.*

status and the reproductive state of the cat. There is also evidence for the existence of clan odors, making it possible for members of a group to identify each other.

Scent, or odor, is also important in stimulating appetite in cats and help them in prey identification. Cats with upper respiratory tract virus infections that cause nasal congestion often will not eat, because they cannot smell the food.

▶ VISION ◀

Cats have good stereoscopic vision and are excellent at detecting movement. Their ability to detect light is three to eight times better than that of humans. Their visual range extends from 10 in (25cm) to 6.5ft (2m), and they have excellent depth perception and blue-green color vision.

Cats are able to see well in the dark, thanks to a special structure (the tapetum cellulosum) that reflects light back onto the retina.

Many Siamese cats have poor stereoscopic vision, and also reduced close vision and flicker detection as a result of an inherited defect. Many of these cats have obvious squints.

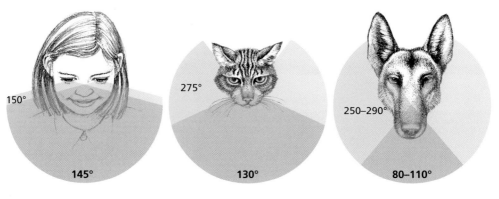

A human has a visual field of 150° from side to side, of which 145° is binocular overlap.

A cat has a visual field 275° from side to side, of which 130° is binocular overlap.

A dog has a visual field of 250–290°, with 80–110° of overlap – much less than that of humans.

Top: *Scent is an important means of communication for cats. It is used to detect territorial boundaries and to find out more about other cats in the area. This cat is displaying the 'gape' response – a lip-curling expression also known as flehming – which delivers the chemicals of the scent to the sensitive vomeronasal organ.*

▶ SOUND ◀

Cats are very sensitive to high frequency sounds of about 60khz. This enables them to detect the ultrasonic squeaks of rodents. They are good at judging the height of a sound's origin, and the mobile external ear (pinna) helps them to locate the source of sound. In addition to their acute hearing, cats have vibration detectors in their feet, which make it possible for them to detect frequencies as low as 200 to 400hz – but only for short periods of time.

▶ VOCALIZATION ◀

Cats scream when attacked or frightened, yowl and wail menacingly when warning off intruders, meow loudly for attention and chirrup a greeting to familiar animals and people (which can sometimes become a prolonged exchange).

Purring usually occurs during relaxed and pleasant experiences, such as suckling or being stroked, although it is sometimes done during times of stress or severe illness. Cats never purr when they are asleep.

Top: *Cats have excellent night vision, which is partly due to the tapetum cellulosum, which reflects light back onto the retina.*

▸ BEHAVIOR PROBLEMS ◂

The feline socialization system is very effective, and cats rarely exhibit seriously problematic or aggressive behavior, unless they have not been de-sexed or are in overcrowded conditions.

Nevertheless, when cats do sometimes exhibit behavior problems, it is usually possible to deal with them because the behavior can be interpreted and responded to appropriately.

STATUS-RELATED AGGRESSION

Some cats are dominant by nature and need to feel in control. They will often growl at or bite owners for no apparent reason. Often this happens while they are sitting on the owner's lap, being stroked. They will suddenly tense up, their pupils will dilate, their tail may lash, and they will bite or take hold of the owner's hand in their teeth.

Such a cat may even attack if the owner has been petting it and then decides to move the cat in order to get up, or just decides to change position without displacing the cat.

DEALING WITH STATUS-RELATED AGGRESSION

Watch for the signs of impending aggression. Stop stroking the cat as soon as it becomes tense, stand up without touching it and let it fall to the floor. A water pistol or horn may be used to startle it out of attack mode.

PREVENTING STATUS-RELATED AGGRESSION

There is no way to prevent status-related aggression from developing. You will have to accept that these cats will never be cuddly – they will always need to be in control.

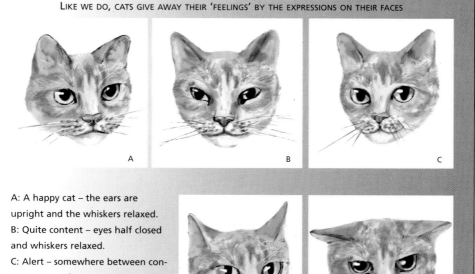

LIKE WE DO, CATS GIVE AWAY THEIR 'FEELINGS' BY THE EXPRESSIONS ON THEIR FACES

A: A happy cat – the ears are upright and the whiskers relaxed.
B: Quite content – eyes half closed and whiskers relaxed.
C: Alert – somewhere between contentment and nervousness.
D: Nervous – the ears move back and the whiskers slightly forward.
E: Angry and frightened – ears flat, eyes narrow, whiskers forward.

UNDERSTANDING YOUR CAT

REDIRECTED AGGRESSION

Cats are masters at 'taking it out' on others. If a cat sees another intruding onto its territory, but cannot get into a position to drive it away (for example, if the cat is locked inside and sees the intruder through a window), it will redirect its aggression onto whoever is close to it – and that might even be you!

If you approach the cat while it is growling at the trespassing cat, it is quite likely to turn around and attack you.

Redirected aggression can also happen if the cat is frightened; for instance, if something falls off a shelf and startles it, at the same moment that you enter the room, the cat may associate you with the frightening experience and attack you.

DEALING WITH REDIRECTED AGGRESSION

The best thing to do is to walk away and leave the cat to calm down. Do not attempt to approach or pacify the cat, because it will remain reactive for a long time in these situations. If the cat continues to react negatively towards you, you may need the help of a behaviorist to overcome the problem. Anti-anxiety medication may be required, along with a behavior modification program.

PREVENTING REDIRECTED AGGRESSION

Avoid approaching your cat if it is reacting to something outside. Never rush to comfort your cat if something has fallen near it or if, for instance, a sudden noise has startled it.

Top: *An arched back and fur standing on end indicate fear or aggression. This is designed to make the cat seem larger and therefore more intimidating. Kittens practice these postures in play.*

PREDATORY AGGRESSION

Some cats will attack people as if they were prey – they stalk and attack quite savagely. The behavior is especially dangerous when directed toward elderly people or children.

DEALING WITH PREDATORY AGGRESSION

When the cat begins to stalk, startle it by using a foghorn or a water pistol. Try to avoid situations that are known to provoke it, such as wiggling your toes inside your socks or sandals or children wearing dangling ribbons or untied belts. Some cats will lie in wait for owners coming to breakfast or follow any other regular routine. Try to vary your routine so that the cat cannot predict where and when you may pass by in order to ambush you.

PREVENTING PREDATORY AGGRESSION

Do not encourage predatory behavior in kittens – for example, do not play games of 'hide and seek' or encourage your kitten to chase you.

Place a bell on the cat's collar so that you may be warned of its approach. (This is not infallible, though, as cats can learn to move without ringing the bell.)

PLAY AGGRESSION

This is seen most often in hand-reared kittens. The lack of contact with littermates means that they do not have the opportunity to learn from retaliating playmates to inhibit their biting or to sheath their claws while playing. These cats can bite hard enough to draw blood, although they have no intention to injure.

DEALING WITH PLAY AGGRESSION

When the kitten or cat starts to elicit play, by batting at your hand or jumping at your feet, redirect the attack onto a toy. If the cat insists on body contact, use a water pistol to discourage rough play. Squirt the cat in the face and say 'ouch'.

Top: *This kitten is preparing to pounce on a playmate – a posture also seen in hunting.*

Reward quiet, gentle play with treats such as pieces of cheese or cat biscuits. Never encourage these cats to chase hands or toes, even if these are hidden beneath blankets, as they will probably bite straight through.

PREVENTING PLAY AGGRESSION

Ensure that young kittens are socialized with other kittens or adult cats. Discourage play involving human body parts such as hands, feet, and toes becoming mock prey.

FEAR AGGRESSION

Cats or kittens that have not been exposed to humans early in life are often fearful of people and may be aggressive when approached. Such a cat will back away, crouch, or lie over on one side and hiss with ears flattened and pupils dilated. It will attempt to escape contact, but will bite if this is prevented.

This sort of behavior is often seen in kittens from wild colonies that people have decided to adopt. It can also sometimes occur in a cat that is being re-homed after its single elderly owner has died. Cats may also show fear aggression when taken out of their home environment, for instance to a vet clinic or cattery.

DEALING WITH FEAR AGGRESSION

With wild-born kittens or re-homed isolated cats, fear aggression can usually be overcome with enough time and patience. However, some wild-born kittens are genetically fearful

Top: *Kittens develop physical skills through play and practice techniques required for self-defense in later life.*

and may never be cuddly pets. Accept them for what they are and respect their independence.

Keep the cat in a room with a litterbox, a bed, a dish of water, and plenty of toys. Spend time in several sessions every day just sitting in the room beside the cat or reading. Reading aloud often helps. Take tasty, strong-smelling cat food with you and attempt to hand-feed the cat. At first you will probably just have to drop the food nearby, but gradually the cat should move closer and closer until the food is taken directly from the hand. Avoid eye contact at this stage.

Do not attempt to touch the cat until it is relaxed when eating from your hand. Gradually entice the cat to play, using paper and string or a flexible stick. Most cats will respond within two to four weeks. Once they can be petted and are relaxed in your company, they can be allowed access to the rest of the house and, finally, to the garden.

Do not attempt to pick up one of these cats until they are completely relaxed, which will probably not happen before at least three months after adoption. In severe cases, they may need anti-anxiety medication.

With pet cats in strange surroundings, it is best to try to desensitize the cat gradually to the whole experience.

First ensure that the cat is comfortable with its carry cage. Feed it in the cage from time to time, and reward it for allowing you to place it in and remove it from the cage. If your cat responds to the herb catnip, place some in the cage. Play with the cat's favorite toy in and out of the cage.

If the cat is fearful of the veterinary clinic, arrange with your vet to bring the cat in regularly and allow it to investigate the rooms and to be fed there. If the cattery is a problem, see if the owners will allow you to do the same thing there. Most cats will eventually learn to tolerate, if not exactly enjoy, these necessary and unavoidable visits.

Above: *Fear aggression is shown by this cat's crouched posture and flattened ears.*

UNDERSTANDING YOUR CAT

AGGRESSION TOWARDS OTHER CATS

Cats are territorial by nature, and will naturally threaten and drive off intruders. It is not really possible to modify this behavior, but you can reduce the chances of your cat being involved in territorial disputes by keeping it indoors at night, in the early morning, and late evening, because these are the times when most disputes are likely to occur.

AGGRESSION TOWARDS OTHER CATS IN THE HOUSEHOLD

Cats living together in a household frequently have minor disputes that are settled by a hiss and a swat with a paw. Usually they can sort it out among themselves and will at least form a truce, if not a loving friendship.

Some cats do become very attached to each other, and wash and groom each other and sleep together. In other cases, though, there is constant and extreme aggression shown towards a cat by one of its housemates. This may be associated with defense of territory (an area in the household that the cat defends as its own). It can, however, also result from redirected aggression.

DEALING WITH INTER-CAT AGGRESSION

Where cats are showing extreme aggression, it is necessary to separate them. Confine them to separate rooms, and swap them daily so that each remains in contact with the scent of the other cat. Teach them both to accept being in a carry cage and feed them in this. Play with each cat at a set time every day, and offer treats.

After a week, bring the cats out at feeding time, in their cages. Place them at opposite ends of a room (not one of the rooms in which they have been kept) and feed them both in their cages. At the first sign of reactivity, remove the offender from the room. Once the

Top: *These two cats are involved in a typical aggressive encounter. Note how the cat on the left is more dominant – its ears are less flattened and it has a more upright posture.*

cats accept being caged at a distance in the same room, gradually move the cages closer together. Once they can quietly sit and eat at a distance of 5–10ft (2–3m) from each other, feed them out of their cages.

If all goes well, place them both on harnesses and leads and sit in the room with them, keeping them at a distance from each other. Any sign of aggression should be reprimanded using a foghorn or a water pistol, and calm behavior should be rewarded. If they are coping, start a series of play sessions using their favorite toys and involving both cats. Eventually they will be able to remain free in the room together, preferably with toys and definitely under supervision. Any aggression should be instantly reprimanded. With time the cats should be able to coexist happily or at least without constant fighting.

Above: *Kittens love to play with wool and fabric, but unfortunately some develop a habit of eating the material as well. This can cause digestive upsets and should be prevented.*

UNDERSTANDING YOUR CAT

DEALING WITH REDIRECTED INTER-CAT AGGRESSION

Redirection of aggression towards other cats occurs in the same way as described for redirection towards people (see p73). The difference is that the cat against whom the aggression is redirected tends to become terrified of the aggressor. When the two cats meet, the victim shows signs of fear, which reinforces the aggressive response in the other cat. These cats should be dealt with as described for inter-cat aggression, although the victim will probably need anti-anxiety medication to stop it from behaving in a way that triggers aggression in the other cat. The aggressor sometimes also needs medication. This situation can be difficult to deal with and the advice of an animal behaviorist should be sought.

FABRIC EATING

The majority of cats are highly fastidious in their eating habits, and most of them are reluctant even to try new foods once they have become used to a certain brand. Some cats, however, can develop bizarre tastes, and one of the most common of these is for fabric.

For some reason, fabric eating is most frequently seen in Siamese cats – it is possible that there might be a genetic predisposition to this behavior among that particular breed.

Fabric eating has also been associated with early weaning, as it is sometimes displayed by kittens who have been removed from their mother and litter mates too early. It can sometimes also be triggered by a traumatic event such as moving house. Fabric-eating cats have even been known to steal woollen clothing from the owner's neighbors, drag it home and suck and chew at it. They may eat large amounts and as a result can suffer digestive upsets and blockages.

DEALING WITH FABRIC EATING

Try to prevent any access to woollen fabric, and perhaps encourage these cats to rip up cardboard. You could also give them bones or rawhide to chew on.

Some cats will stop eating or chewing fabric if you apply an aversive substance such as chilli or pepper to the fabric. It may also help simply to increase the amount of attention you give to your cat. Spend some quality time with it and try to provide more stimulation such as games and new toys.

Some vets believe that these cats may suffer from an underlying neuro-chemical abnormality, so medication may be required.

PREVENTING FABRIC EATING

Try to avoid using woollen bedding for kittens. Provide plenty of stimulation and activity and avoid early weaning of kittens. Avoid purchasing kittens from fabric-eating parents.

HOUSE SOILING

Many people experience problems with house soiling during their cat-owning lives. There are several possible causes.

Any cat living inside should have access to a clean litterbox. If it is free to enter and leave the house, it may never use one, but if the weather is cold and wet, or for some reason it feels apprehensive about venturing outside, it is useful to have a litterbox. In multi-cat households there should be one litterbox per cat, and one extra. These boxes should be changed daily if soiled. Types of litter include bark, woodfibre, sawdust, sand, clay, clumping (scoopable), 'flushable', recycled paper pellets, and granulated absorbent pellets. Perfumed substances are sometimes available.

Trays should be big enough for the cat to turn around in, and with sufficient depth of litter to allow digging. They should also be stable, because if they wobble the cat will feel insecure.

SOILING NEAR THE LITTERBOX

This is usually a problem related to the type of litter in the box, or to an association of pain or unpleasantness with using the litterbox. Often the paper around the box will be scratched up in an attempt to dig and cover.

DEALING WITH SOILING NEAR THE LITTERBOX

Check that no other cat has been using the box, as most cats resent sharing, and ensure that the box is kept clean and fresh. Some cats may not like perfumed litter. If there is no apparent problem, have the cat checked by a veterinarian. It may have a bladder or bowel problem that has caused it to anticipate pain with getting into the box. If it is an old cat it may have arthritis, making it uncomfortable to climb into the box and balance.

If the cat is healthy, consider changing the type of litter. Offer the cat several types of litter in different boxes and see which one, if any, it uses. Place the boxes in different areas to which the cat has ready access and in which you would be happy for the litterbox to stay permanently if need be. Rotate the litter types so that you have tried all types in all possible areas. The reason for this is that it may not be a litter problem – it may be that the cat has been chased by another cat or otherwise disturbed while digging in the box and so is afraid to climb into it in that area. If you cannot solve the problem, consult an animal behaviorist.

PREVENTING SOILING NEAR THE LITTERBOX

Ensure that there are always enough clean litter trays for each cat, plus one extra.

URINATION IN THE HOUSE

Cats may urinate in other parts of the house because:

O they have cystitis (a bladder infection)
O they have a litter aversion (*see above*)
O they are afraid to use the litterbox because it is in a high-traffic area and they are frequently disturbed
O another cat has used the box or another cat chases or otherwise intimidates them when they try to approach the box
O they are marking part of the house as their territory.

Urine may be sprayed from a standing position or deposited from a squat.

Spraying is not usually associated with ill health. It is a way of marking territory or of expressing aggression by cats that do not have the confidence to engage in direct conflict. Cats that are spraying or urinating in the house are often very anxious.

DEALING WITH URINATION IN THE HOUSE

Take the cat to the vet for a check-up. Confine the cat to one easily cleaned room when you cannot supervise it, and provide a litterbox. If the cat doesn't use the box while in the room, treat as described for soiling near the litterbox.

If the cat is using the litterbox in the room, gradually reintroduce it to the rest of the house, having cleaned all previously soiled areas with an enzymatic cleaner. Do not allow the cat to be anywhere unsupervised. If it attempts to dig, squat, or spray, squirt it with a water pistol or alarm it with a foghorn, but do not physically or verbally abuse it.

If the cat is marking territory, it may be that the social relationships between the cats in the household have somehow changed. Marking is often seen when a new cat is introduced to the household. In a single cat household, marking may be done in response to a visitor staying for a few days or a new partner moving in. It can also occur in response to the presence of cats outside the house, and as a reaction to strange cats entering the house. Try to identify any major triggering factors. For example, if the cat is urinating or spraying on the windowsill it is probably reacting to the presence of a strange cat outside. Fitting blinds to the window and keeping the cat out of the room when these are not closed may solve the problem. If you have seen strange cats hanging around, invest in a cat door that is electronically operated by a trigger on your cat's collar. This ensures that no other cat can enter.

If you feel that the cat may be stressed by changes that have occurred within the household, try to provide it with extra attention and some stability by playing a game with it at a fixed time daily. This helps to reduce anxiety.

These problems can be difficult to solve and you may need the help of an animal behaviorist to identify the cause of the problem.

PREVENTING URINATION IN THE HOUSE

Ensure that strange cats cannot enter the premises and that there are enough clean litter trays. Try not to change the home environment suddenly. Introduce the cat to new housemates before they move in and take things slowly. Take care to introduce new cats or other new pets to the cat gradually, too. Provide some routines and ensure that each cat has a special place to which it can retreat, such as a shelf on a cat tree, cupboard, or cardboard box where it will feel safe.

DEFECATING IN THE HOUSE

Cats use feces as a territorial marker – this is known as middening. Feces are coated with a secretion from two glands situated on either side of the anus, which contains information about the cat which other cats will receive when they sniff at the feces. Where disputes are happening frequently it is not uncommon for cats to use feces in addition to urine to make a point. Other reasons for defecating in the house include litter aversion as described on the previous page, ill health, and poor house training.

DEALING WITH AND PREVENTING DEFECATION IN THE HOUSE

Follow the same protocol as for urination in the house. There may be underlying stress factors and an animal behaviorist should be consulted if the problem continues.

Top: *Litterboxes should be clean, roomy, and placed in an area allowing some privacy.*

HUNTING

Cats are natural predators. Even kittens that are hand-reared in total isolation may still grow up to be effective hunters. Prey includes birds, rodents, and lizards. It is not uncommon for cats to bring their prey home to present to their owner. Many people find predation by their cats unacceptable. This is especially true in areas where cats may prey on endangered wildlife.

Dealing with hunting

Since cats do most of their hunting early in the morning, in the evening, or late at night, keeping them confined at these times will greatly reduce their predatory behavior.

The only way to prevent it completely is to keep your cat confined inside continuously. Cats can and do adapt to this lifestyle, provided they are given plenty of stimulation through play and companionship.

Other methods of reducing predation include placing a collar and bell on the cat and the application of startle tactics such as foghorns whenever the stalking cat is observed. These methods are not very successful, though. Cats soon learn to position themselves in such a way that bells will not sound during a stalk, and although startle tactics may prevent a cat from targeting the bird table they will do nothing to reduce predation in other areas when it is far away and out of sight.

Some collars produce a series of beeps in response to a sudden leap by the cat, but have not proved to be completely successful.

Ensuring that cats are well fed before going out may reduce the amount of predation slightly. However cats are still likely to hunt when well fed – they just won't eat the prey and may play with it for longer prior to killing it.

Preventing hunting

As this is instinctive behavior, cats cannot be taught not to hunt. The only way to prevent hunting, unfortunately, is to deny access to prey.

JUMPING ONTO HIGH SURFACES

Cats enjoy vertical space. Most love to climb trees or any other structure that will give them a good vantage point from which to survey their world. Benches, shelves, tables, fridge tops, and mantelpieces are appealing to cats for this reason. Not only does it enable them to survey their territory, but it also helps them to satisfy their curiosity. This is normal cat behavior, but not all owners find it equally appealing or admirable.

Dealing with jumping onto high surfaces

Cats can be trained not to jump onto forbidden surfaces. Try squirting them with a water pistol as soon as they jump up, or startling

Top: *Try not to apply 'human morality' to cats and regard their instinctive hunting tendencies as cruel – cats are simply honing their inherited hunting skills.*

them with a loud noise. Placing something sticky, but non-toxic, all over the high surface (try honey) may act as a deterrent. A smooth piece of plastic or card that slips easily and will fall off when the cat lands on the surface can be very effective, too.

PREVENTING JUMPING ONTO HIGH SURFACES
○ Train your cat from kittenhood.
○ Don't tantalize your kitten or cat by preparing its food on the counter while it watches hopefully from the floor or nearby chair. Prepare the food while the cat is outside or in another room, and place the food in its feeding area before the cat arrives.
○ Provide your cat with an alternative vertical space of its own, such as a cat tree or a high shelf with its own special bed from which to view the world.

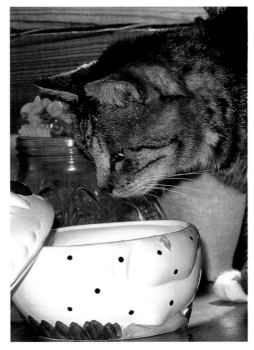

SCRATCHING FURNITURE

Cats scratch as a means of marking territory. The marks provide a visual signal to other cats, and scent from the sebaceous glands in the feet is deposited during the scratching process to further identify the owner of the territory. Favored sites are usually vertical wooden surfaces. Outside, tree trunks and fence posts are the usual notice boards. Inside, furniture will do just as nicely.

DEALING WITH FURNITURE-SCRATCHING
Cats often like to scratch as soon as they wake up, so it is a good idea to provide a scratching post near to your cat's sleeping area.

Scratching posts come in a variety of shapes, sizes, and materials – cats seem to enjoy the ones made of wood and covered with carpet.

Others combine a serrated dense card which can be shredded, or use hessian as a covering.

If your cat insists on using the furniture as a scratching post, there are two main options: either train the cat not to scratch except in certain approved areas, or protect the furniture in some way to reduce the amount of damage that the claws may do. A cat's claws may be trimmed in much the same way as a dog's toenails, and if this is done regularly from kittenhood cats accept the procedure quite happily. Ask your vet to demonstrate how this is done. You will need to trim the claws every four to six weeks. An alternative to this is to apply plastic sheaths to the claws – these are glued on in much the same way that women apply false fingernails.

Top: *Cats are naturally curious and love to explore table tops, especially if they've learnt that they might find food there.*

startle it. Other methods include booby-trapping areas with small balloons, which will pop when scratched and alarm the cat.

PREVENTING FURNITURE-SCRATCHING
Encourage your kitten to use a scratching post – suspend a toy from the post, or place catnip around the post as an incentive (not all cats are susceptible to the lure of catnip, though).

DECLAWING
This must be regarded as an absolute last resort. Declawing is the surgical amputation of the first joint of every digit on the cat's forefeet. It is a mutilation that causes much post-operative pain, and it is possible that declawed cats experience phantom pain throughout life in the same way that human amputees do.

This procedure is illegal in some countries, for example the United Kingdom.

Declawing should never be necessary if owners are prepared to put the time and effort into training their cat not to claw furniture and regularly trimming the claws.

To train your cat not to scratch furniture you need to be vigilant, and the cat must not have unsupervised access to the house. Keep a water pistol handy and squirt the cat as soon as it attempts to scratch, or use a foghorn to

YOWLING AND CRYING

Some cats can be very vocal and seem to 'talk' incessantly. The Oriental breeds are more likely to behave in this way than other breeds. These cats become very attached to their owners and need company – and they are naturally vocal.

Unspayed females of any breed will yowl and cry when in season, and un-neutered males have a special yowl when seeking a mate.

Where vocalization has become excessive or has suddenly started in a previously quiet cat, there may be an associated health problem such as hyperthyroidism or, in an elderly cat, cognitive dysfunction or 'feline Alzheimer's' disease. If the cat is otherwise healthy, it could be a sign of anxiety. If the cat yowls when out of sight of the owner but is quiet in the owner's presence, it could be suffering from separation anxiety (see at right).

DEALING WITH YOWLING AND CRYING
If the problem has started in a previously quiet cat, take it for a complete health check.

If all is well, consider if there have been any major changes in your cat's surroundings or lifestyle that may have upset the animal.

If the cat is yowling and rubbing around you but is quiet when you are not there, it is seeking attention. Try to reserve a special time to spend with the cat each day when it has your undivided attention, is given treats, and is

Top: *Cats prefer to scratch their claws against an upright feature, but if none is available, the horizontal arms of your furniture will do.*

played with. At other times ignore the yowling and pet the cat when it is finally quiet. Provide plenty of interest for the cat in the form of toys for times when it is alone.

If these tactics bring about no improvement, consult an animal behaviorist.

PREVENTING YOWLING AND CRYING

O Ensure that fresh food is freely available from a cat café (automatic feeder) throughout the day.

O Alternate feeding and playing with the cat.
O Install a cat door so that your cat does not have to demand to be let inside.
O Don't rush to the cat whenever it cries.
O Give your cat quality time of play and companionship every day.
O If you are a busy person, consider keeping two cats as company for each other. It is best to get two kittens rather than introduce another cat or kitten at a later stage to an adult animal.

SEPARATION ANXIETY

Cats may become extremely attached to their owners to the point that they are unhappy if left alone. These cats need to have constant owner contact. They cry incessantly when left, even if the owner is in an adjacent room. The condition is seen most commonly in Oriental cats and cats that have been hand-reared.

O Do not carry hand-reared kittens around continuously, but give them time alone with a stuffed toy and hot water bottle.
O Some cats will show this behavior no matter how they are brought up.

DEALING WITH SEPARATION ANXIETY

O Encourage the cat to relate to other members of the family.
O When the cat must be left alone, provide lots of environmental stimulation such as new toys and meaty bones to chew.
O Resist demands for constant attention; choose when you wish to pet the cat.
O Create as much stability and routine in the cat's life as possible.
O In extreme cases, anti-anxiety medication may be required.

PREVENTING SEPARATION ANXIETY

O Ensure that all family members have contact with the cat.
O Do not give in to attention-seeking behavior, supply affection on your terms.

Above: *Cats, especially hand-reared ones, can become extremely attached to their owners, sometimes to the point that they are unhappy if left alone even for short periods.*

6. BREEDING AND REPRODUCTION

▶ A NEW MEMBER OF THE FAMILY ◀

Kittens are cute and delightful, but before deciding to let your mixed-breed cat have a litter, ask yourself how likely it is that you will find good homes for them. Remember that every year thousands of unwanted kittens are destroyed by humane societies.

There is no evidence to suggest that having a litter is physically or psychologically beneficial to your female cat, so don't feel that she is being deprived if she is spayed when she is six months old. If you have six to eight friends waiting eagerly for kittens from your cat, then you can probably allow her to breed with a clear conscience. If your cat is pedigree and you breed her to a pedigree tom, you should be able to place the kittens. Ask the breeder of your cat or the owner of the sire if they have lists of people waiting for kittens.

Above: *While mixed-breed kittens are as charming as pedigree ones, they are more difficult to sell or give away, so think carefully before allowing your mixed-breed queen to mate.*
Opposite: *Cats are excellent mothers.*

If you do decide to breed from your cat, try to delay the event until she is at least a year old. Although cats can breed at six months, they do better if allowed to mature first.

When your cat first comes into season (also called 'coming into heat') you will notice a distinct change in her behavior. She will become excessively friendly, roll around on the ground and yowl in a tone that you have never heard from her before. When rubbed on the back she will raise her hindquarters and tread with her hind limbs.

If your cat is not pedigree and is at the right age to be bred, all you have to do is let her go outside once she is in heat, and a roaming tom cat will quickly find her. Before you do this,

Above: *Pregnant queens usually remain agile and playful until they are close to giving birth.*
Top: *The typical mating sequence. The male holds the female's neck, and as he dismounts, the female will usually turn and spit or hiss at him.*

local cat breeders association. Try to view the tom before sending your cat to him. Make sure the breeder is registered and that the tom is certified free from disease and is fully vaccinated. It is customary to send the queen to the tom because the tom may be distracted in unfamiliar surroundings, and some queens will attack toms that are suddenly introduced to their territory.

Gestation (time from mating to birth of kittens) lasts from 56 to 63 days. During this time the cat should be fed good quality food on demand. Commercial foods are available for pregnant and lactating cats, and it is probably easiest to use these. If you choose to feed a home-prepared meat diet, you will need to provide a calcium supplement. See your vet for advice on this. Your cat should also be dewormed monthly, and treated for fleas with a topical treatment that will not harm the kittens (check with your vet).

however, ensure that she has had all her vaccinations and has been dewormed and treated for fleas.

Cats are induced ovulators, which means that mating triggers ovulation (shedding of the egg from the ovary). They often mate with several toms during their season and as a result the kittens may have different fathers. Once a female has been successfully mated, she will stop showing signs of heat.

If your cat is pedigree, you will need to keep her indoors because tom cats from miles around will camp on your lawn and fight under your windows. Other bad news is that your female will come into season every three weeks from late winter/early spring until she is mated.

To arrange for a suitable mate for her, consult the breeder of your cat or contact your

During your cat's pregnancy, get her accustomed to the area in which you would prefer her to give birth. This may be a specially prepared box or basket in a spare room or the bottom of a wardrobe. She needs a place where she can feel secure and relaxed, and it should also be easy to keep warm and clean. It is helpful to have her sleeping in this area throughout her pregnancy.

▶ GIVING BIRTH ◀

About 12 hours before giving birth your cat will seem restless and agitated. She may eat less than usual, and may vocalize and seek human company. Encourage her to stay in the kittening area, and if necessary sit with her as time permits and encourage her to relax.

Eventually the birth contractions will start, and at this stage most cats are best left alone. Check on her every 20 minutes, or allow one person to remain in the room with her. Some

cats, especially Oriental types, may panic during labor, especially if it is their first. They may abandon their kittens and follow their owner around crying. These cats may need to be sedated, so it is best to contact your vet.

Kittens are born at varying intervals, most within 30 to 60 minutes of each other. Occasionally several hours may lapse between kittens. If the cat is not distressed and is not straining, you need not be concerned. If she

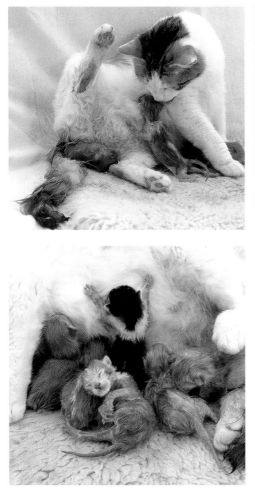

seems weak or distressed and is not interested in the kittens she already has produced, call the vet. If she is straining for longer than 20 minutes and no kittens are produced, seek veterinary assistance immediately.

Cats are wonderful mothers and rapidly clean the kittens and eat the placenta (afterbirth). Many cats purr blissfully throughout the whole procedure. If your cat doesn't clean the kittens at the time of birth, you will need to intervene. Use clean hands to clear the membranes from around the kitten's mouth and a rough towel to firmly rub its body. Holding the kitten head-down helps to allow fluid to drain out of its airways.

▶ REARING ◀

The kittens should feed naturally within 10 to 20 minutes of birth. If any seem to be having difficulty then have them checked by your veterinarian. Allow your cat unlimited access to food and water while she is feeding the kittens.

Kittens can start on solid food at two to three weeks old. Provide commercial kitten food for them. You can also offer commercial kitten milk. Do not offer them cow's or goat's milk because these contain the milk sugar lactose which the kittens may not be able to digest properly.

Provide two litterboxes and change them regularly during the day. Kittens will naturally

Top: *The birth process – giving birth, eating the afterbirth, and suckling the kittens.*

start using litterboxes from three to four weeks. Until then, the queen will keep them, and the nest, clean.

Your nursing cat should be dewormed monthly and the kittens should be dewormed every two weeks until they are three months old, starting at two or three weeks. Flea treatment of the mother should also be continued during feeding, using a product that is non-toxic to the kittens. The kittens will not need separate treatment until they are weaned.

Kittens may be weaned from seven to eight weeks old. Your cat will be spending less time with them by this stage and they will be taking lots of solid food.

It is important that kittens have human contact between two to seven weeks or they will be shy or aggressive towards people and it will be less easy to find them a home. The more exposure they have to novel, non-threatening stimuli, including other animals and noises, the more easily they will settle into their new homes.

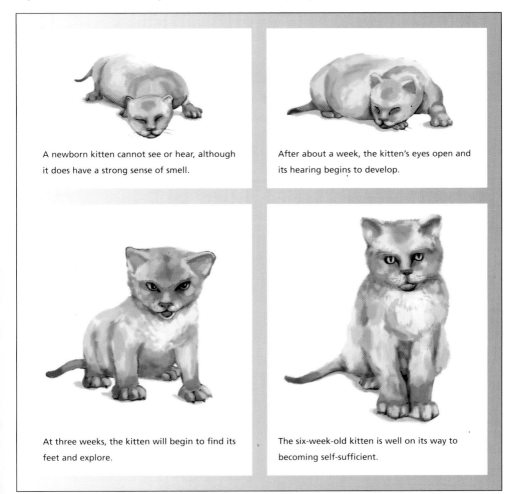

A newborn kitten cannot see or hear, although it does have a strong sense of smell.

After about a week, the kitten's eyes open and its hearing begins to develop.

At three weeks, the kitten will begin to find its feet and explore.

The six-week-old kitten is well on its way to becoming self-sufficient.

Top: *The development of a kitten's senses*

7. THE MATURE CAT

▶ A HAPPY RETIREMENT ◀

During the last couple of decades the average life expectancy of pet cats has increased by at least two years, largely the result of better nutrition and health care. There are now more elderly cats in the feline population and, like elderly humans, they need special care.

▶ SIGNS OF OLD AGE ◀

With increasing age always comes a gradual deterioration in health and, while nothing can be done to stop the aging processes, it is possible to minimize its effects. So take note of the signs of old age, and give your cat the extra care it deserves.

CHANGES TO COAT AND CLAWS

Most cats don't develop many gray hairs as they get older, but the aging process tends to cause their coat to grow longer, even in short-hair breeds. As their joints become less mobile they become increasingly less able to groom themselves properly, so that their formerly smooth and sleek coat begins to look unkempt, with the fur 'broken' open. Their claws grow more quickly so nail trimming is required more frequently.

DEEP SLEEP

Another sign of old age is increasingly deeper and more prolonged sleep. Old cats are more likely to be startled if woken suddenly, and some cats may even hiss or spit if you wake them unexpectedly by even by gently touching or stroking them.

- O Allow your elderly cat to sleep peacefully in places of its choice, where it can relax undisturbed and in comfort.
- O Warn children in the household not to disturb or startle it.
- O Keep other pets away as much as possible.

Above: *Older cats need extra care and may appreciate regular combing.*
Opposite: *A portrait of your pet is a wonderful memento of the times you shared.*

CHANGES IN FEEDING AND DRINKING PATTERNS

Your older cat may experience a loss of appetite or a reluctance to eat – it could have difficulty in eating or drinking, too. These symptoms are commonly associated with gum inflammation (gingivitis), tartar formation, or tooth decay, which are common problems in elderly cats.

An older cat may also experience increasing thirst. This may be a sign of a developing kidney disease or some other health problem.

Old cats may benefit from an adjustment to their diet – changing to foods that are more easily digested. Many vets recommend a diet that contains lower protein levels, to lessen any stress on the kidneys. Not all vets agree, so talk to your practitioner, who may recommend a special therapeutic diet.

It is a good idea to take your cat for frequent health checks and routine blood samples to monitor its kidney and liver functions.

WEIGHT LOSS

Weight loss can occur over a period of several months, even though the cat is still eating well, but you might not notice it because the weight loss is gradual. One cause may be an overactive thyroid gland, a condition that can be treated, so don't just accept it as an inevitable part of aging.

Top: *Coat color changes can occur as part of the aging process (just as people turn gray), though these changes can also indicate poor health.*

DIGESTIVE PROBLEMS

As a cat ages, it may experience tooth or gum problems that make it difficult to chew, and its digestive system may not function as efficiently. Symptoms of digestive problems include vomiting of food or bile-stained (yellow-green) saliva, diarrhea and constipation. These may respond to:

○ feeding three to four small meals daily (as for kittens)

○ including a greater proportion of moist foods in the diet

○ feeding products containing more easily digested forms of protein (for example lightly boiled egg yolk)

○ changing to a prescription diet on the advice of your vet.

ARTHRITIC CHANGES AND OSTEOARTHRITIS

An early sign of arthritis and osteoarthritis is stiffness when getting up and on first moving around in the morning; this stiffness improves as the day progresses and the animal's joints and muscles warm up. In more extreme cases the cat has difficulty walking, with weakness of the hind legs, lameness and symptoms of pain.

Two-thirds of osteoarthritis cases in cats are first recognized by their owners, so as soon as you notice any signs you should talk with your vet and follow his or her advice.

Treatments include:

○ a non-steroidal, anti-inflammatory drug, which can be given daily in tablet form for long-term treatment

○ drugs that aid the production of joint fluid

○ various homeopathic and natural remedies are available that can be tried, including green-lipped mussel extract, herbal remedies, and shark cartilage.

Top: *Some cats cope better with old age than others. This cat has survived well into its 20s, with an excellent quality of life.*

REDUCED BLADDER CAPACITY AND LOSS OF BLADDER CONTROL

A very old or arthritic cat has a reduced bladder capacity. One of the earliest signs of this may be frequent visits outside or to the litterbox. In the later stages it may begin to lose control over its bladder (urinary incontinence), and small amounts of urine may leak onto the places where it sits, lies, or sleeps. Ensure that it always has a clean litterbox indoors.

CONSTIPATION

An old cat has more difficulty in passing feces, and these may be passed at irregular intervals. Arthritic changes may also prevent it from adopting a normal excretory posture. Because cats usually defecate outside, you may not notice these symptoms for some time, so as your cat begins to age you should try to keep a closer watch on it.

If constipation develops, talk to your vet about possible corrective measures, which may include the addition of small amounts of medicinal paraffin to the cat's food or a change to a prescription diet.

Above: *Older cats appreciate extra warmth and comfort, as they tend to spend a large part of their day asleep.*

INCREASING DEAFNESS

In the early stages deafness may be difficult to detect, because it occurs gradually and many cats learn to adapt. One of the first signs may be failure to respond to your usual calls.

As your cat's hearing deteriorates it will be more prone to accidents. It may not hear vehicles that drive onto your property or approach it on the road.

INCREASING BLINDNESS

The same principles apply as when making a household safe and comfortable for humans losing their sight. Avoid moving furniture, and protect the cat from danger. A partially or even completely blind cat can usually live a contented life as long as it feels safe and can live undisturbed in familiar surroundings.

Deteriorating sight may not be detected during its early stages. Watch out for the following:

O the eyeballs appear a bluish color (the cornea is affected)

O the eye appears white in the center (a sign of cataract)

O the cat starts to blunder into objects such as furniture

O the cat is reluctant to go out at night and/or into bright sunlight.

SENILITY

Signs of senility are:

O disorientation
O restlessness
O increased demand for your attention
O increased vocalization.

Just like elderly people, old cats have good days and bad days. As the 'owner' you will have to adapt, and be tolerant and sympathetic to the cat's needs. As the situation progresses you will probably need an increasing amount of advice and involvement from your veterinarian, and medication may be required.

▶ CARING FOR AN ELDERLY CAT ◀

You can reduce stress on your aging cat by following these suggestions:

O Put comfortable blankets or rugs in its favorite lying places, out of full sun and away from damp areas.

O Protect it from situations in which it is likely to fall: for example, put barriers across steps or stairs, and make sure that it cannot fall from a deck or balcony.

O If it shows less interest in eating, then slightly warm the food or change the diet to something more palatable.

O Adjust its food intake according to its level of activity. As a cat takes less exercise it tends to put on weight, which makes it more prone to heart disease. Ask your veterinarian about diets specially formulated for health conditions such as aging kidneys.

O Monitor how much water it is drinking. If the quantity is increasing, talk to your vet.

O Take your cat for regular health checks. Booster vaccinations need to be kept up to date, and teeth and gums checked. Routine blood sampling may assist with health care.

O If you have to go away, arrange for a housesitter or an alternative home environment rather than a cattery.

▶ THINKING ABOUT A REPLACEMENT ◀

As your cat begins to age, you may decide to bring another cat or a kitten into the household. You will need to spend a little time integrating the two animals and working at preventing inter-cat aggression, but it creates a transitional stage that may help you cope with the impending loss of an old friend while adapting to the different demands of a kitten or young cat.

You may decide to wait because nursing an old cat may be enough to cope with, without having to take time away from this older companion to spend with a younger one.

Above: *It is important to involve all the family members in decisions about euthanasia, as everyone needs time to say goodbye.*

If you are in any doubt about what to do, talk to your veterinarian and the veterinary nurses at the clinic. They will have plenty of experience of owners who have been through the same difficult situation as you, and should be able to offer sound advice. Whenever you get a replacement, you will have to decide what sort of cat to get, which will be influenced by whether your mature cat is still around – and both of you will need to adapt to the new individual.

▶ THE FINAL DAYS ◀

This can be the most difficult period of your whole relationship with your cat, yet in many ways it can be one of the most rewarding times, too. This is your final opportunity to repay the companionship that your cat has given to you during the happy times you have spent together. If you know what to expect during these remaining days, you will find the inner strength to cope with them and know that your care and concern are being noted.

As your cat becomes more frail, its reliance on you will increase, and nursing procedures will take up more of your time.

As its sense of smell deteriorates, your cat will be less able to detect the aroma of foods, and will therefore become more fussy about what it eats. You will need to talk to your vet about the problem, and try out different types of food to discover what the cat prefers. Loss of bladder and bowel control may result in 'accidents' to clean up, and if the cat sleeps in a basket its bedding may need frequent changing and washing.

Increasing deafness and blindness will make life more difficult for both of you, and your cat may become disoriented and demand more attention from you day and night.

Give your cat that attention. Physical contact, and the message of love that it carries, is very important; so spend as much time as necessary gently stroking and cuddling your cat to let it know that you are there, and how much you care. Sometimes an old or dying cat will purr a lot more. Why this happens is not fully understood, but for the owner it can be a comforting sound during what is often a stressful time.

▶ MAKING THE DECISION ◀

Sometimes the final decision is made for you, and the cat dies suddenly and naturally.

In most cases there is no such solution and you, the owner, will have to make the decision to authorize euthanasia. It may come easily, or you may find it very difficult. We witness death (human and animal) on television, videos, and films many hundreds of times every year, yet most of us have been brought up in a society that does not cope particularly well with dying, and are unprepared for it in real life. If there are children in your family, discuss the situation with them and allow them to express their emotions, their feelings and views about it. Talk about the positive aspects that came from owning the cat, and explain that however good their health care may be, cats have a much shorter life expectancy than we do.

The overriding factor in your decision must be to do what is best for the cat, not for yourself or your family. That decision will probably be made with the help of your veterinarian, who can play an important role as a counselor and adviser.

Veterinarians and their staff understand what you are going through. They deal with this situation almost every day, and many of them have been through a similar situation with a cat of their own. They understand your grief and sense of loss, but also know that they can end your cat's suffering in a humane way. It is a treatment option.

▶ THE GRIEVING PROCESS ◀

Grieving is a natural human reaction to the death of a much-loved cat or other pet, and you need to express it. There are five well-documented stages in the grieving process, and you will pass through each of them to some degree or another.

1. Denial and depression. Confronted with the fact that your cat is at the end of its life, you will probably suffer from depression to a greater or lesser extent. It is often at the subconscious level, and not immediately apparent to those around you. You may tell yourself, 'They've got it wrong', 'Things may not be as bad as they seem', or 'There must be something else that can be done'. This reaction cushions your mind against the emotional blow it is experiencing.

2. Bargaining. In the human grieving process this involves offering some personal sacrifice if the loved one is spared. It is less likely to happen when a pet is involved, but you may still say things to yourself such as, 'If you get better I promise to let you sleep on my bed.'

3. Pain and anger. Your emotional pain and feeling of frustration evokes anger. This may be directed at somebody else, such as a close relative or your vet, or it may be directed at yourself, and emerge as a feeling of guilt. At this stage the support of your vet may be particularly helpful, because negative feelings are not constructive and need to be replaced by positive thoughts.

4. Grief. By this stage the feelings of anger and guilt will have gone. Your cat has died, and all that remains is a feeling of emptiness. The less support you get at this stage, the longer that feeling will last. If support doesn't come from your family or friends, then get it from another source, such as your veterinarian or a professional counsellor. People who don't own pets may not understand and it is best not to discuss it with them.

5. Acceptance and resolution. It will take time – on average three to four months – but eventually your grieving will come to an end. Fond memories will replace grief, and appreciation will replace the sense of loss. Your deep feelings for your cat will remain, but now they will be positive as you recall the happy times the two of you spent together. You may even celebrate them by obtaining a new pet.

Knowing the stages of the grieving process, and how your family, friends and the staff at your veterinary clinic can help, should enable you to come through the event with a minimum of pain and a maximum of love.

Our pet animals have a shorter life span than we do, and on average an owner will suffer the loss of a dearly loved pet five times or more during a lifetime. Each time such a loss occurs, the owner will experience grief. It doesn't get any easier the more often it happens, for each pet is an individual and the owner grieves individually for it.

▶ EUTHANASIA ◀

The usual procedure for euthanasia is the injection of an overdose of anesthetic into a vein. There is no pain, and the cat falls asleep within 15–20 seconds. You may wish to be present during this procedure, or you may prefer not to witness it and say your last farewell afterwards. The choice will be yours.

Your veterinarian and the veterinary nurses who have assisted will understand what you are going through, and your tears are a natural reaction. One of their obligations is to help you deal with your grief. Remember, if people did not love their animals so much, the veterinary clinic and its staff would have a much reduced function.

▶ BURIAL OR CREMATION ◀

Your veterinarian can help you to decide what to do next and, if necessary, find somebody who can help to make arrangements. You may wish to have your cat cremated, in which case a casket or urn containing the ashes can be returned to you. This can be buried, or kept. If you wish your cat to be buried, it can be done in your garden or in a pet cemetery.

▶ COUNSELLING ◀

For some pet owners the lingering grief can become intolerable. If this should happen to you, do not suffer in silence – seek help from others. This may come from a traditional counselling service, or from social workers at veterinary teaching institutions who are specially trained to counsel pet owners in all matters, including the loss of a pet. Once again, your veterinarian should be able to advise you.

Top: *The joints of an older cat become less flexible, and it is not able to reach every part of its body with its tongue for grooming. Its once glossy coat therefore begins to look 'broken open'.*

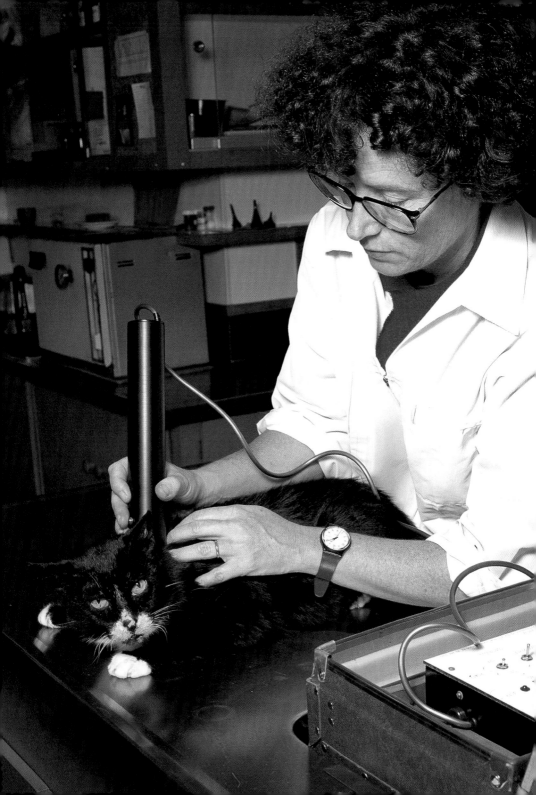

8. PROTECTING YOUR CAT'S HEALTH

▶ THE VETERINARY CLINIC ◀

To keep fit and well your cat needs regular health care. Some of it will be provided by you, and some will require the skills of a professional. Veterinary clinics are not just centers for the treatment of ill health. They are also a valuable source of practical information, specialized products, and friendly advice from veterinarians and their trained nursing staff.

Most veterinary clinics also act as valuable community resource centers, providing information about local boarding facilities, cat groomers or cat-sitting services, for example. Many also have notice boards on which their clients can post information, such as photographs of missing pets, or kittens looking for a new home.

The changes in veterinary science over the years, and particularly during the last decade, have been remarkable. In addition to radiography (X-rays) and routine blood sampling, modern diagnostic aids include ultrasonography (the use of ultrasound scanning equipment), Magnetic Resonance Imaging (MRI) and Computer Assisted Tomography (CAT) scans.

Certain methods of diagnosis and therapy – some ancient, some new – are also now becoming a recognized part of a comprehensive approach to animal health care. Known as Complementary Veterinary Medicine (or Complementary and Alternative Veterinary Medicine – CAVM), many of these methods have been used in human medicine for years, but their integration into veterinary practice has been comparatively recent. For example, some veterinarians are now trained in veterinary acupuncture and acutherapy (the examination and stimulation of specific points using acupuncture needles, injections, low-level lasers, magnets and a variety of other techniques for diagnosis and treatment); veterinary chiropractic (the examination, diagnosis and treatment through manipulation and adjustments of specific joints, particularly the vertebrae, and of areas of the skull); massage therapy; homeopathy; botanical medicine, nutritional therapy and even the use of flower essences (diluted extracts from certain flowers).

Other modern areas of veterinary specialization include:

O Anesthesia
O Orthopedics
O Ophthalmology
O Endocrinology
O Dermatology
O Animal Behavior
O Dentistry
O Medicine
O Surgery
O Radiology
O Diagnostic imaging

Opposite: *Painless laser therapy can be effective in relieving muscular aches and pains and can speed up the healing of ligament injuries.*

▶ THE IMMUNE SYSTEM ◀

The bodies of animals, like those of humans, have various defense mechanisms to protect them against disease caused by micro-organisms in the environment.

Healthy skin acts as a physical barrier, while the mucous membranes in the nose, trachea and bronchi help to trap foreign substances and prevent them from entering the lungs. Other primary barriers include acid in the stomach, which kills many invading organisms, and mucus produced from the lining of the intestines. The liver destroys the toxins produced by bacteria.

These defense mechanisms work well when an animal is healthy, but are less effective if it suffers malnutrition, is weakened in any way, is unhealthy, or mentally or physically stressed.

Most organisms that cause disease consist mainly of proteins. If an organism gets past the primary barriers, the body quickly detects these 'foreign' proteins and produces antibodies against them. Antibodies are produced by specialized white blood cells found mainly in the lymph nodes and spleen. They circulate in the blood and are usually very specific, destroying only the organism (the antigen) that stimulated their production.

The first time the cat's body encounters a specific disease, introduced from the environment or by means of a vaccine, it may take up to 10 days to produce antibodies. The next time the disease is encountered, antibody production occurs very rapidly, preventing the disease from becoming established.

Antibody levels wane with time, but if the antigen is encountered again (either through infection or a booster vaccination), antibody production immediately resumes. Immunity created by vaccines is not generally as long lasting as the 'natural immunity' which the body establishes for itself when it is exposed to a disease and manages to fight it off. This explains why booster vaccinations may be needed to keep an animal protected.

PASSIVE (MATERNAL) IMMUNITY

Passive immunity is established when a newborn animal acquires antibodies from its mother. It does not produce antibodies, but acquires those which the mother had produced against disease to which she had been exposed.

Newborn animals have a very rudimentary immune system that takes many weeks to develop fully. To tide them over this period they receive passive immunity from their mother in the form of antibodies, some of which enter their body while they are still in the uterus, but most of which are taken in with the mother's colostrum, or first milk. This is a critical period for the newborn animal, which can only absorb these antibodies during the first day or two after birth.

If a queen has a prolonged kittening or gives birth to a large litter, the early kittens will have more opportunity to ingest colostrum than those born later, so the degree of passive immunity may vary between littermates.

A queen can only pass on antibodies to those diseases that she herself has encountered, or against which she has been vaccinated. Therefore a queen that is not vaccinated, or lives in isolation from other cats, will have fewer antibodies to pass on, and her kittens will be more vulnerable from birth. A queen used for breeding must be vaccinated, and her booster vaccinations kept up to date.

Passive (maternal) immunity is only temporary. Passive immunity wanes over time, the amount of antibodies in the blood halving every seven days or so. In most kittens the level of maternal immunity will have fallen almost to zero by the age of 12 weeks.

ACTIVE IMMUNITY

Active immunity is the result of an animal producing antibodies from its own immune system, in response to disease or vaccination.

To be protected, kittens must develop their own, active immunity, either by contact with a specific disease or through vaccination.

While its passive immunity is still high, the kitten is protected from disease, and its own immune system may not respond to a vaccination. Some brands of vaccine are designed to override it though, and stimulate the kitten's immune system.

Although we know that the level of passive immunity steadily decreases, we cannot be sure at what age each individual kitten will entirely lose this immunity and respond to vaccination. In some kittens this can occur much earlier than 12 weeks, so these will be at risk if they are not vaccinated and are exposed to a virus.

The typical recommendation for a kitten from a queen that has been properly vaccinated is to receive two vaccinations, the first at eight or nine weeks of age and the second (booster) four weeks later. In areas of high risk, vaccination may be started at six weeks of age and repeated at two week intervals until 12 weeks. Your vet will advise you if this is necessary.

Top: *Kittens receive antibodies in their mother's milk, which protect them against certain diseases until they are between six and 12 weeks old.*

▸ VACCINATING YOUR CAT ◂

In many countries, routine vaccination programs have greatly reduced the incidence of several important feline diseases. Many different brands of vaccine are available, including multiple (combined) vaccines that are effective against several diseases. Your veterinarian will advise you which vaccines are the most suitable for your cat.

▸ FELINE RESPIRATORY DISEASES ◂

Many different organisms can cause respiratory infection in cats, but there are two in particular that are equally responsible for about 90 per cent of all cases of respiratory infections in cats, and for the disease complex that is commonly called feline influenza or cat flu.

Feline herpesvirus-1 is a virus similar to the one that causes cold sores in humans.

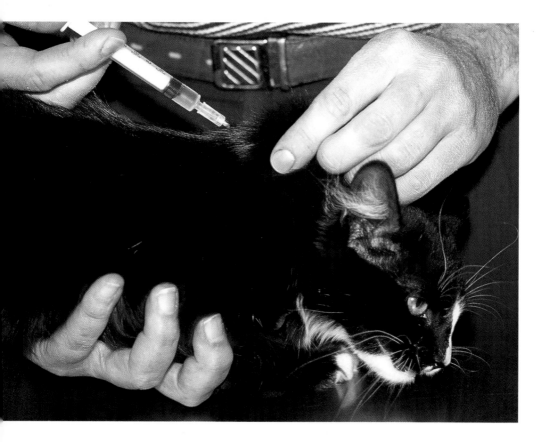

Above: *Soon after you get your new cat, register it with your local vet, who will keep up-to-date records of vaccinations and booster dates.*

The disease that it causes is called feline viral rhinotracheitis (FVR), and is highly contagious. Initial signs are sneezing, fever, and a discharge from the eyes and nose that quickly becomes purulent due to secondary infection by bacteria. As the disease progresses, an affected cat may develop ulcers in the mouth, bronchitis, and eventually pneumonia. A pregnant queen may abort her kittens. Although not many adult cats die from the disease, the death rate among kittens can be 50 to 60 per cent. Recovered cats often carry the virus for years. Much of the time they are not infectious to other cats, but every now and again they go through episodes during which the virus is shed.

A similar percentage of feline respiratory infections are caused by feline calicivirus (FCV). In these cases ulceration in the mouth, nose, and on the tongue, is common. Other symptoms are similar to those of FVR, although the disease may be less severe. Recovered cats become carriers of the virus, which may then be persistently shed.

Respiratory infections due to a combination of both the above viruses are not uncommon.

About five per cent of respiratory infections are caused by Chlamydia psittaci, an organism called a 'rickettsia' that is classified as intermediate between a virus and a bacterium. It causes a disease that was once called feline pneumonitis and, unlike the viruses mentioned above, will respond to certain antibiotics. It causes runny eyes (conjunctivitis) and nose (rhinitis), although fever or more severe respiratory symptoms are uncommon, and deaths are fortunately rare. It can be particularly troublesome where there are groups of cats, such as in boarding catteries or breeding establishments.

Above: *Heart murmurs are common in cats, and a heart check should be part of your cat's annual check-up.*

▶ FELINE INFECTIOUS ENTERITIS (FIE) ◀

Also known as feline panleucopenia (FPL), this was once one of the most common and widespread of serious diseases in domestic cats. As a result of vaccination programs it is now well under control. The disease causes a dramatic drop in the numbers of circulating white blood cells, and symptoms include fever, loss of appetite, vomiting, depression, and diarrhea. Kittens are most susceptible and there is a high mortality rate. Even cats that survive this debilitating disease often remain weak and vulnerable for the rest of their lives.

▶ FELINE LEUKEMIA VIRUS (FELV) ◀

This is the most important cause of feline cancer. Symptoms are variable, and can include vomiting, diarrhea, lethargy and labored breathing.

Various types of treatment may be tried, including chemotherapy, but these are often unsuccessful. FeLV affects one to two per cent of cats, but the disease is more common in some countries than others.

OTHER VIRUSES

Two other nasty viruses are feline infectious peritonitis (FIP) and feline immunodeficiency virus (FIV).

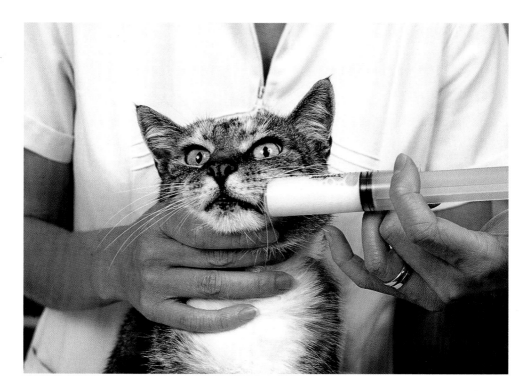

Above: *The easiest way in which to administer liquid medicine is with a syringe.*

PROTECTING YOUR CAT'S HEALTH

▶ RABIES ◀

In countries where this viral disease is endemic, cats are routinely protected by vaccination. Rabies can affect any mammal and is almost always fatal. Transmitted through the saliva of infected animals, usually the result of a bite, it can also be spread by infected saliva coming into contact with mucous membranes (eye, nose or mouth) or a skin wound.

In Europe foxes are the most important carriers, while in North America raccoons, bats, skunks, foxes, and coyotes are the culprits. In Mexico and other Latin and Central American countries, cats are the most common carriers.

The incubation period is usually two to eight weeks, but can be up to six months. The virus travels via the nerves to the brain where it causes inflammation (encephalitis) resulting in recognizable nervous symptoms. In the last stages of the disease, the virus moves into the salivary glands and saliva. In its early stages, rabies commonly causes changes in behavior and personality. Affected animals become anxious and increasingly sensitive to noise and light. Nocturnal animals may be seen out during the day, and wild animals may lose their fear of humans. A normally timid cat may for instance become more friendly, while a normally friendly cat may become shy and hide away from light.

As the disease progresses, affected cats may become restless and irritable, and they are likely to attack other animals or humans without provocation. They eventually develop paralysis of the throat and cheek muscles, which makes it impossible for them to swallow – as a result, saliva drools from their mouth. Breathing becomes increasingly difficult, and in the final stages the animal collapses, enters a coma, and dies.

PREVENTION

In certain countries where rabies is endemic their law requires the vaccination of cats and dogs. Many island nations, in which the disease is not endemic, have strict quarantine laws to prevent its introduction. In Britain, a scheme has been introduced that allows vaccinated cats and dogs entry under certain conditions (see PETS Travel Scheme, pp49–50).

If your cat fights with any mammal that is a rabies carrier, saliva carrying the virus could be present on that cat's coat or in any of the wounds inflicted on it.

If you think your cat has been in a fight with a rabid animal:

O Take extreme care when handling your pet. Use gloves, and cover it with a towel.
O Allow as few people as possible to handle it.
O Call Animal Control or an equivalent organization.

O Don't try to capture the attacking animal.
O Take your cat to a veterinarian.
O If your cat does not receive a booster within 72 hours then, unless the attacking animal tests negative, your cat will have to be quarantined for six months at a veterinary clinic or disposed of by Animal Control.

If you are bitten or scratched by an animal you suspect is rabid, or if its saliva enters an open wound or comes into contact with your nose, eyes or mouth, wash the wound or contact area using household detergent or soap. These kill the virus faster than any disinfectant. Get immediate medical attention – treatment involves a course of vaccinations.

Take these routine precautions to prevent rabies:

- Don't feed or attract wildlife into your yard.
- Call Animal Control if you suspect there is a rabid animal in your yard. Don't try to capture wildlife.
- Don't allow bats to live in your attic or chimney.
- Don't pick up dead or abandoned animals.
- If you are particularly at risk (for instance, if you regularly handle dead animals or nerve tissue), ask your physician if you should be vaccinated.

▶ EXTERNAL PARASITES ◀

External parasites live on or in the skin of the cat. Most external parasites are host-specific, which means that they infect one particular species of animal only – among the exceptions is the cat flea, which may also infect dogs. However, host-specific fleas will also bite humans.

Above: *Flea powders and flea collars have now been largely superseded by easy-to-use topical liquid preparations.*

PROTECTING YOUR CAT'S HEALTH

FLEAS

Most cats are likely to become infected with fleas at least once during their life. Sources of infection include other cats, dogs, hedgehogs, and even rabbits. The flea most commonly found on cats is the cat flea (*Ctenocephalides felis*).

The major natural factor controlling the flea population is not so much the temperature, but the humidity, because the cat flea cannot develop if the humidity is less than 50 per cent. In winter, even with central heating, the humidity is around 40 per cent, so fleas are less of a problem. In summer, humidity and air temperatures rise, so the flea population increases.

The most common symptom of flea infestation is repeated scratching, and nibbling or licking at its fur – some cats may even become skittish and edgy, as if they are trying to run away from their fleas. Fleas occur in greater numbers on some areas of the body than others; especially along the back just in front of the tail. You can see if there are any fleas present by grooming the cat with a flea comb, which will comb out either the live fleas or their droppings (flea dirt). To identify the latter, squeeze them between two pieces of damp tissue. They contain digested blood, which will stain the tissue reddish-brown.

Cat fleas remain on a cat only long enough to feed and lay eggs. The latter quickly fall off into the environment, and contaminate the cat's bedding and the household. Flea control must include treatment of all pets and the household. There are new topical preparations available in single-application packaging that are quick and simple to apply, even to cats, requiring only a few drops to be placed between the shoulder-blades. There is also a product available in pill form or as a single-dose liquid in a squeeze tube – which is very easy to administer – that interrupts the life cycle of fleas feeding on the cat.

TICKS

These are more common in rural areas, and often attach to a cat's head or neck. To remove them, swab them with denatured alcohol (methylated spirits) for a short time, grip them as close to the skin as possible with a pair of tweezers, then pull them off. Some ticks (particularly in Australia) are toxic and can kill small animals such as cats. Your local vet will have up-to-date information.

Top: *A not-too-unusual friendship – introduce a kitten to this little family pet and they could become great companions. However, guinea pigs and cats can transmit fleas to one another.*
Above: *Fleas are external parasites that stay on the cat only long enough to feed and lay eggs.*

MITES

The ear mange mite (*Otodectes cynotis*) results in irritation that causes the cat to scratch at its ears. In doing so often introduces a secondary bacterial infection, and the ear becomes inflamed and painful. If your cat often scratches at its ears, get a vet to check them. Treatment usually involves ear drops or an ointment. Use a product prescribed by your vet.

A very small mange mite (*Notoedres cati*) may burrow into the skin, especially around the sides of the face and between the eyes and ears. It causes irritation and skin thickening, and scratching and licking by the cat results in hair loss and baldness. This type of infection can take some time to treat, and veterinary advice is essential.

The larvae of the harvest mite (*Trombicula autumnalis*), variously called red bugs or chiggers, can infect cats during the summer and early autumn. They are usually found on less furry areas of a cat's skin, such as the ears, sides of the mouth, and between the toes. Various insecticides are available, so talk to your veterinary clinic.

Fur mites (*Cheyletiella* species) are common on cats, dogs, and rabbits – each type of animal has a specific mite species. These mites may cause itching, but the most common sign is profuse dandruff, especially along the cat's back and sides. Although not particularly serious to cats, this mite can also infect humans, on whom it causes itchy welts and blisters that progress to dry scaling. Areas most commonly infected are the hands and forearms, and sometimes the chest.

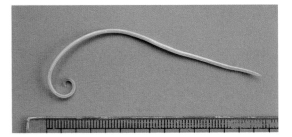

The sarcoptic and also the demodectic mange mites are quite common on dogs, but these are rarely seen on cats.

LICE

Healthy cats are unlikely to become infected, but debilitated or sick cats may contract an infection because they are unable to groom themselves properly.

The lice (*Felicola* species) lay white eggs (nits) that are firmly attached to the hairs. Various insecticides are available for the treatment of this condition.

▶ INTERNAL PARASITES ◀

Regular veterinary checks (including, if necessary, examination of fecal samples) and regular deworming should ensure that your cat does not suffer from these internal parasites. Ask your vet clinic for advice about the treatment procedures best suited to your cat's particular infestation.

Above: *When infected by the roundworm* Toxocara cati, *adult cats show few signs of ill health.*
Top: *The most common mange mite to infect the cat is the* Otodectes cynotis.

ROUNDWORMS

The ascarid worms, *Toxocara cati* and *Toxascaris leonina*, are the most common roundworms in cats. They can grow up to 4 in (10cm) long, and lay eggs that under suitable conditions can remain viable in the environment for years.

Infection may be direct (from eggs) or indirect (from eggs that have hatched into infective larvae in an intermediate host such as a mouse or rat).

In most parts of the world, about one cat in every five is infected with *Toxocara cati*. While infected adult cats may show few, if any, signs of ill health, the larvae of this worm can infect suckling kittens via the mother's milk, and kittens can be seriously affected.

HOOKWORMS

These tend to be a problem in warmer and more humid areas. They are most common in Australia, New Zealand, parts of the United States, and South Africa, but less so in the United Kingdom. The *Ancylostoma* species is the most important, and a heavy infestation can cause severe anemia and even death. Veterinary treatment is essential.

Top: *Getting their own back: mice infected with tapeworm (*Taenia taeniaeformis*) will transmit the parasite to their killer, the cat.*

TAPEWORMS

The most common tapeworms in cats are the *Dipylidium caninum*, transmitted by a cat eating infected fleas or lice during grooming, and *Taenia taeniaeformis*, transmitted by a cat eating infected prey such as rats or mice.

Above: *Avoid direct contact with cat feces, as it can transmit a number of parasites, such as the protozoan* Toxoplasma gondii – *wear rubber gloves as a precaution.*

Top: *Tapeworm segments may be shed in a cat's feces, or adhere to the fur at the rear end.*

PROTECTING YOUR CAT'S HEALTH

WHIPWORMS (TRICHURIS) AND THREADWORMS (STRONGYLOIDES)

These parasites are mainly found in the warmer, more humid parts of the country as well as in Australia, and are rarer in cats than in dogs. The life cycle is direct.

FLUKES

Areas of risk are mainly North America and tropical regions. Most infections are the result of cats eating raw fish. Veterinary treatment is possible.

LUNGWORMS

A number of different species of lungworm can infect cats, but not all of them cause serious problems.

Aleurostrongylus abstrusus needs veterinary treatment, though, and symptoms range from mild coughing to severe breathing problems.

HEARTWORMS

Although more common in dogs, heartworms are parasites that can infect cats, especially in warmer parts of the United States around the Mediterranean and Australia. Signs include coughing and breathlessness, and sudden death may occur. Treatment is essential.

TOXOPLASMOSIS

Infection by the protozoan *Toxoplasma gondii* rarely causes symptoms in cats, but the significance of this parasite lies in the fact that the disease can be transmitted to humans through the feces of infected cats. Pregnant women are particularly at risk. Simple precautions include wearing rubber or cotton gloves when emptying a litterbox, avoiding contact with cat feces and washing hands after handling the cat. Children's sandboxes should be covered.

FELINE INFECTIOUS ANEMIA (FIA)

The incidence of this disease varies in different parts of the world. It is caused by *Haemobartonella felis* (or *Eperythrozoon felis*), a protozoan parasite transmitted by biting insects such as mosquitoes. The parasites destroy the red blood cells, and early symptoms include pale mucous membranes and lethargy. The disease is usually noticed by the cat's owner during its early stages, and can be treated with antibiotics. However, it is often associated with feline leukemia virus (FeLV) and in these cases the chances of recovery are poor.

Above: *The fungal infection ringworm causes bald patches on the cat's skin, and is highly contagious to humans.*

9. MONITORING YOUR CAT'S HEALTH

▶ SIGNS OF ILL HEALTH ◀

The earlier you can detect a health problem and do something about it, the better. Treatment is more likely to be effective, and your cat will probably suffer less discomfort or pain. Learn what is normal, so that you can detect when something abnormal occurs.

▶ EARLY SIGNS OF ILL HEALTH ◀

One of the first signs of ill health may be a subtle change in your cat's usual behavior. It may be quieter than usual, less active, or disinclined to go for a walk. It may be more thirsty, or less hungry. Since cats, like humans, have their 'off' days, you should keep an eye on this sort of change for a day or two. If it continues, then take further action.

Consult your veterinarian if your cat shows:

O unusual tiredness or lethargy
O abnormal discharges from the nose, eyes, ears, or other body openings
O excessive head shaking
O excessive scratching, licking, or biting at any part of the body
O markedly increased or decreased appetite
O excessive water consumption
O difficult, abnormal, or uncontrolled waste elimination
O marked weight loss or weight gain
O abnormal swellings on any part of the body
O abnormal behavior such as hyperactivity, aggression, or lethargy
O lameness
O difficulty in getting up or down.

As soon as you see anything unusual, make a note of it, for you may need this information if you take your cat to a veterinarian at a later date. Doctors talk to their human patients to get a 'history' of their problem before making an examination and reaching a diagnosis. Vets cannot ask their animal patients about the problem, and rely on their owners for such a 'history'.

Above: *Kittens should be vaccinated against infectious diseases at eight or nine weeks old, and as adults they will need annual boosters.*
Opposite: *Chiropractic treatment is one of many alternatives to traditional veterinary medicine.*

▶ PAIN ◀

Pain results from the stimulation of specialized nerve endings (receptors) in the body. It has many causes, but is usually the result of injury, infection, poisoning or inflammatory reaction. It is one of the earliest signs of disease.

When we suffer pain, we can tell somebody. A cat cannot speak, but in most cases your cat's reactions will be fairly clear to you.

○ It will usually cry out in pain if you accidentally step on its foot or if something strikes it. It may cry out if you touch a painful part of its body, and even hiss, bite, or lash out at you.
○ If it has hurt a leg it may put its foot on the ground but place no weight on it, limp, or carry the leg off the ground.

○ If it is suffering from joint pain, for example from arthritis, it may cry out when getting up or lying down.
○ Pain or irritation from its anal glands will cause it to 'scoot' its bottom along the ground. In response to hind-end pain it may frequently inspect the affected area.
○ Pain in an eye will cause it to paw at the affected area or rub it against objects.
○ Pain in an ear usually results in it tilting its head to the affected side and shaking it.
○ Mouth pain may cause it to salivate and shudder its jaws.

It can be more difficult to detect when a cat is suffering spinal, head, or internal pain. The only indication that something is wrong may be a less obvious change in its behavior.

SUSPECT SPINAL PAIN

If your cat:
○ seems to be lame, but no limb is affected
○ resents being touched along its back
○ humps its back and/or trembles when standing up
○ is incontinent
○ has difficulty assuming the normal posture for defecation
○ collapses on its hindquarters.

SUSPECT HEAD PAIN (HEADACHE)

If your cat:
○ has half-closed eyes, but has no obvious eye problem
○ presses the top of its head against objects
○ gently, but regularly shakes it head
○ stares vacantly in a manner you haven't noticed before.

SUSPECT INTERNAL PAIN

If your cat:
○ spends more time lying down
○ is particularly restless, and unable to settle down
○ keeps its abdominal muscles tensed or stands in a hunched-up position
○ continually strains to have a bowel movement, but fails to do so
○ is usually docile and becomes inexplicably aggressive whenever you or another animal comes near it.

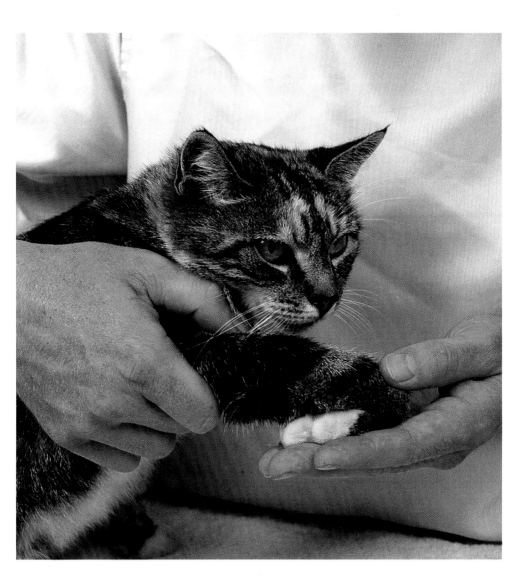

WHAT TO DO

If the pain was caused by a minor accident (for example, somebody stepped on the cat's paw), use common sense and monitor the outcome. If the pain persists after a few hours, you should contact your vet.

If pain is the result of something more serious, or if you are not able to determine the cause, you need to seek advice from your veterinarian without delay. Do not merely guess and hope for improvement while the cat suffers.

Top: *There is not always an obvious reason for lameness. Your veterinarian is the best person to determine the cause.*

BLOOD AND CIRCULATORY SYSTEM PROBLEMS

SIGNS	SOME POSSIBLE CAUSES	ACTION
Exercise intolerance, lethargy, weakness, fainting (kitten or young cat)	Congenital malformation in which blood bypasses the lungs	Take to the vet in each case
As above, poor growth, distended abdomen	Congenital defect in which blood bypasses the liver	
As above (any age)	Heart valve defect	
As above (any age)	Anemia	
Coughing	Congestive heart failure (chronic heart disease) Heart-based tumor Heartworm disease (see p115)	Take to the vet in each case
Abnormal breathing	Lung congestion due to poor heart function Warfarin poisoning Anemia	ALL URGENT. Take to the vet
Pale or bluish tinge to gums	Warfarin poisoning Poor heart function Abnormal destruction of red blood cells Blood clotting disorder	Take to the vet in each case
Jaundice (yellow tinge to gums and whites of eyes)	Abnormal destruction of red blood cells Secondary to liver infection	Take to the vet in each case
Abdominal distension	Fluid accumulation due to poor heart function	Take to the vet
Loss of use of hind limbs, howling, hind feet feel cold	Aortic thrombosis (blood clot blocking one or both femoral arteries)	URGENT. Only about half of cats recover with treatment

EAR PROBLEMS

SIGNS	SOME POSSIBLE CAUSES	ACTION
Shaking head, scratching ears, blackish discharge	Ear mites	Take to the vet
Shaking head, reddish or yellowish-white smelly discharge from ear. Ear painful to touch	Inflammation of ear canal and inside ear flap. External ear infection (otitis externa), usually caused by a mixture of bacteria, fungi and yeasts. Can cause severe pain and discomfort and lead to permanent ear damage	Do not place anything into the ear, as drum may be ruptured and some treatments may be harmful if they enter the middle ear. Vet will check ear drum (tympanic membrane) is intact, and may take a swab to determine which infective organisms are present. Follow the treatment prescribed by your vet
Head tilted to one side, loss of balance, abnormal movement of eyeballs (nystagmus). Cat may be shaking head	Middle and inner ear disease (otitis media and otitis interna). A foreign body penetrating the ear drum, or chronic ear infection	Take to the vet. Treatment may involve anti-inflammatory drugs, antibiotics, and drugs to stop vomiting
Scabs on white ears	Sunburn (white cats are particularly susceptible)	If the scabs are superficial and skin is reddened, it is probably sunburn. Apply pediatric sunblock three times daily. Keep cat out of intense sunlight
	Cancer of the ear (squamous cell carcinoma). White cats are particularly susceptible	If the scabs are deep, long-standing and have never healed, it may be skin cancer. Take to the vet. Treatment may involve freezing with liquid nitrogen or surgical removal

ENDOCRINE PROBLEMS

SIGNS	SOME POSSIBLE CAUSES	ACTION
Abdominal enlargement, excessive thirst, symmetrical hair loss, pigment changes	Hyperadrenocorticism or Cushing's syndrome (excessive production of adrenalin)	Take to the vet
Excessive thirst, increased appetite and urination, weight loss (middle-aged or old cat)	Diabetes mellitus	Take to the vet

SIGNS	SOME POSSIBLE CAUSES	ACTION
Neck swollen, hyperactive, increased appetite, vocalization and urine output, excessive thirst, weight loss	Hyperthyroidism (excess of thyroid hormone)	Take to the vet

EYE PROBLEMS

SIGNS	SOME POSSIBLE CAUSES	ACTION
Avoiding light, blinking	Several	Take to the vet
Runny eyes, clear discharge	Wind, dust, strong sunlight, allergy or blocked tear duct May have no tear duct	Bathe with cooled, boiled water or ophthalmic saline If it doesn't clear, take to the vet
Runny eyes, clear or purulent discharge, whites of eyes inflamed, pawing at eyes	Bacterial or viral conjunctivitis	Take to the vet
As above, one eye only	Possible foreign body in eye, or injury	Take to the vet
Tacky, purulent discharge, eye surface dry, conjunctiva inflamed	Dry eye (keratoconjunctivitis sicca)	Take to the vet
Eyes appear to be white, cat's vision affected	Cataract formation	Take to the vet
Cat appears blind, no other symptoms	Retinal degeneration	Take to the vet
Closing one eye, avoiding light, eye watering, blood in the eye	Inflammation within the eye (uveitis)	Take to the vet
White line or dot on eye surface, pain, eye watering	Corneal ulcer, often result of a cat scratch	Take to the vet
Third eyelid showing	Nerve damage	Take to the vet
Pressing head against objects, eye protruding, avoids light	Glaucoma (swelling of the eyeball due to accumulation of fluid)	Take to the vet

INTESTINAL PROBLEMS

SIGNS	SOME POSSIBLE CAUSES	ACTION
Eating well, but thin	Worm burden	Treat for worms
Vomiting and/or diarrhea (may be intermittent), weight loss	Inflammatory bowel disease (IBD) – the inflammation of the bowel and a reduction in its ability to absorb nutrients May be bacterial overgrowth Because affected cats are not obtaining enough protein, they may lose weight	Take to the vet
Flatulence	Usually dietary More common in kittens	Talk to vet about changing diet
Chronic weight loss despite normal or increased appetite	Worms, intestinal tumor, inability to absorb nutrients	Talk to vet to confirm cause
Vomiting, not eating	Inflammatory bowel disease (see above)	Take to the vet
Hunched-up posture	Foreign body Severe constipation Abdominal pain	Take to the vet in all cases
Straining to defecate, hard firm feces, straining ceases after passage of feces, not vomiting	Mild constipation, particularly common in elderly cats and longhaired cats	Give one teaspoon medicinal paraffin (mineral oil) If feces are not passed within eight hours, take to the vet
Straining to defecate, few/no feces, depressed, possibly vomiting	Severe constipation	Take to the vet to ascertain cause
Diarrhea, one or two bouts, without blood, cat otherwise bright and alert, no vomiting	Food intolerance Mild bacterial enteritis	Water only for one day, then bland diet for 24 hours If diarrhea stops, gradually re-introduce diet If continues, see vet
As above, after cat has drunk cow's milk	Lactose intolerance	Feed commercial low-lactose milk
Diarrhea, frequent and persistent, cat otherwise bright	Giardiasis (Giardia infection) Coccidiosis	Take to the vet in each case

SIGNS	SOME POSSIBLE CAUSES	ACTION
Diarrhea, frequent, may be blood present, depressed, abdominal pain	Bacterial enteritis (e.g. Salmonella or Campylobacter) Colitis, tumor	Take to the vet in each case

LIVER, SPLEEN AND PANCREATIC PROBLEMS

SIGNS	SOME POSSIBLE CAUSES	ACTION
Abdominal distension, with or without jaundice	Liver tumor	Take to the vet
Vomiting, jaundice, dark-colored urine, abdominal pain, poor appetite	Bile duct blockage Bile duct rupture	Take to the vet in each case
Vomiting, diarrhea, jaundice	Feline infectious peritonitis (FIP)	Take to the vet
Acute, persistent vomiting, fever, abdominal pain	Pancreatitis. Pancreatic digestive enzymes are secreted into the pancreatic tissue, causing inflammation and tissue destruction Can cause death Recovered animals may suffer permanent dysfunction of the gland	Take to the vet
Excessive thirst, hunger, possibly abdominal enlargement, lethargy, weight loss	Diabetes mellitus. If the pancreas does not produce enough insulin, glucose levels build up in the bloodstream Glucose then passes through the kidneys into the urine, taking water with it	Take to the vet for blood and urine tests Some cases may be controlled by adjusting the diet; most cases require insulin injections given at home
Cat wobbly and uncoordinated, may progress to depression Cat 'spaced-out' May bump into things If not treated, will collapse	Hypoglycemia (low blood sugar) due to too much insulin or too little food	Inadequate glucose levels in the bloodstream are further lowered by the action of the injected insulin, leading to collapse, coma and convulsions Treatment is to give glucose or honey by mouth. Owners of diabetic cats should always keep these substances on hand in case of an emergency

SIGNS	SOME POSSIBLE CAUSES	ACTION
Very depressed and prostrate The breath may smell like nail polish remover (acetone)	Ketoacidosis (build-up of ketones in the bloodstream) may occur if the diabetes is not properly controlled and blood sugar reaches excessively high levels	Take to the vet
Cat comatose	May be either ketoacidosis or hypoglycemia	URGENT ACTION Take to the vet Do not attempt to treat at home

MOUTH AND ESOPHAGUS PROBLEMS

SIGNS	SOME POSSIBLE CAUSES	ACTION
Bad breath	Tartar build-up on teeth	Take to the vet Teeth may be scaled and polished under anesthetic
Bad breath, bleeding gums, difficulty in eating	Gingivitis (inflammation of gums)	As above
Difficulty in eating, bad breath, jaw shuddering, dribbling	Broken or infected tooth	Take to the vet for tooth extraction Other teeth may need attention
Drooling, pawing at mouth, may be gulping	Foreign body (e.g. bone or stick) lodged across the hard palate, or fish hook in lip Cut tongue (due to fighting or licking out of cat food tin)	If possible, open mouth and check Remove foreign body if possible Otherwise, take to the vet
	Bee sting in mouth (on tongue, inside cheeks or gum)	If possible, open mouth and check Remove sting with tweezers Check mouth regularly, and if more than slight swelling take to the vet
	Ulcerated tongue	If tongue inflamed or ulcerated, investigate access to irritant poisons Take sample of suspected substance to the vet
Drooling, retching or coughing	Object stuck in throat	If possible, open mouth and check Remove foreign body if possible Otherwise, take to the vet
	Tumor in mouth	Take to the vet

SIGNS	SOME POSSIBLE CAUSES	ACTION
Loss of balance, uncoordinated	Middle ear infection Vestibular disease (infection, inflammation or tumor affecting the vestibule) Brain tumor Disease of cerebellum	Take to the vet in each case
As above, and cat's diet contains raw fish	Thiamine deficiency	Take to the vet for thiamine injections, and change the diet
Muscle spasms, fits or convulsions	Epilepsy Poisoning Brain tumor	Take to the vet
Muscle spasms, fits or convulsions during late pregnancy or within 8 weeks of giving birth	Eclampsia (lowered calcium levels in bloodstream)	URGENT ACTION Get vet treatment with calcium injection
As above, may be head pressing, pain around head	Encephalitis or meningitis	URGENT ACTION NEEDED Take to the vet
Collapsing, third eyelids visible, limbs rigid, tail straight, facial muscles contracting	Tetanus infection	Take to the vet
Salivating, may be other signs	Poisoning	Take to the vet in each case
Salivating, behavioral change	Rabies	Take to vet (see also p109 and p143)
Abnormal head position, eyes may be flicking from side to side	Middle ear disease Vestibular disease (infection, inflammation or tumor affecting the vestibule) Brain tumor	Take to the vet in each case
Collapsing in hindquarters, with or without acute pain	Disc protrusion in thoracic or lumbar region	Take to the vet
Collapse, walking in circles or partial paralysis, eyelids partly closed, eyes flickering	Stroke	Take to the vet

REPRODUCTIVE PROBLEMS IN THE QUEEN

SIGNS	SOME POSSIBLE CAUSES	ACTION
Persistent estrus	Ovarian cyst	Take to the vet
Excessive thirst, reduced appetite, vomiting, distended abdomen, vulval discharge, 6–8 weeks after end of estrous cycle	Pyometra (accumulation of pus in uterus)	URGENT ACTION Take to vet Surgical removal of uterus and ovaries may be necessary
Enlarged mammary gland, not painful or painful and inflamed	Mammary tumor (not always malignant) Mastitis	Take to the vet in each case
Lethargy, appetite loss within 1–2 weeks of kittening. May be purulent discharge from the vulva	Metritis (inflammation of uterus)	Take to the vet May need antibiotics or spaying

RESPIRATORY SYSTEM PROBLEMS

SIGNS	SOME POSSIBLE CAUSES	ACTION
Sneezing, clear nasal discharge	Viral infection Allergy (e.g. to pollen) Blade of grass lodged in nose Feline viral rhinotracheitis (FVR) Feline calicivirus infection (FCV)	If persistent, take to the vet in each case
Sneezing, purulent nasal discharge from one or both nostrils	Tumor Bacterial or fungal infection Molar abscess	Take to the vet in each case
Red, puffy skin on nose, with some crusting	Allergy (e.g. to mosquito bites) Sunburn Early skin cancer	If red and sore, keep out of the sun Apply pediatric sunblock If does not subside, take to the vet
Noisy breathing	Laryngeal problem (e.g. laryngitis) Allergic bronchitis	Take to the vet

SIGNS	SOME POSSIBLE CAUSES	ACTION
Rapid breathing	Pneumonia Heart problem Allergic asthma Poisoning (e.g. aspirin) Ruptured diaphragm after fall or accident Pyothorax (pus in chest, usually the result of a cat bite)	Take to the vet URGENT Take to the vet in each case
As above, gums pale or white	Internal or external hemmorrhage Poisoning (e.g. warfarin)	URGENT ACTION Take to the vet in each case
Choking, collapse	Foreign body in throat obstructing breathing	Try to remove the obstruction Take to vet urgently
Abdominal movement associated with breathing	Ruptured diaphragm after accident/trauma Pneumothorax (air in the chest, usually after accident/trauma) Pyothorax (see above) Hemothorax (blood in chest) after poisoning with anti-coagulants (e.g. rat poison) Rib/lung damage from trauma/accident	Take to the vet in each case
Bleeding from nose	Acute trauma Foreign body in nose Problem with clotting mechanism Poisoning with rodenticide (e.g. warfarin) Tumor	Take to the vet in each case
Coughing, mild, occasional	Tracheitis Allergy Heart problem	Take to the vet in each case
Coughing, frequent, shallow, history of accident	Pneumothorax (air in chest)	Take to the vet
Coughing, frequent, harsh, associated purulent nasal discharge, cat appears ill	Feline viral rhinotracheitis (FVR)	Take to the vet

SKELETAL, JOINT, AND MUSCLE PROBLEMS

SIGNS	SOME POSSIBLE CAUSES	ACTION
Slight lameness on one limb, one joint mildly painful when flexed or extended	Sprain (slight damage to ligament or cartilage in a joint)	Get veterinary advice
Sudden lameness, bleeding foot	Cut pad	Take to the vet
Sudden lameness on one hind leg. Touching toe to ground but not bearing weight on it	Ruptured anterior cruciate ligament in knee joint Usually the result of an accident.	Take to the vet This may need surgery
Sudden lameness, holding one hind leg off the ground	Slipped knee cap (patella)	Take to the vet
Sudden lameness, hind limb painful	Hip dislocation Fracture of head of femur	Take to the vet in each case
Sudden lameness after fall or accident, swelling over a section of the affected limb, pain	Bone fracture	Take to the vet
Sudden lameness, swelling of tissue on leg	Bite wound	Take to the vet Wound may form an abscess
Sudden hind limb collapse, probable pain	Fractured pelvis	Take to the vet
Difficulty getting up or down, eases out of stiffness after activity	Arthritis (degenerative joint disease)	Take to the vet
Difficulty in assuming normal posture for urination/defecation	Spondylosis (degenerative condition resulting in deposition of extra bone between vertebrae)	Take to the vet
Firm, painful swelling just above a joint, becoming larger over period of time	Osteomyelitis (bone infection)	Take to the vet
Chronic lameness in one leg	Arthritis (degenerative joint disease)	Take to the vet

SKIN PROBLEMS

SIGNS	SOME POSSIBLE CAUSES	ACTION
Scaly skin, white flakes in coat	Cheyletiella (mite) infection	Ask vet for insecticidal treatment
Flaky, itchy skin on head and shoulders Tiny insects visible	Lice (see p112)	As above
Hair loss, symmetrical, no irritation, no broken hairs	Hormonal imbalance	Take to the vet
Broken hairs and asymmetrical hair loss	Psychogenic alopecia, self-inflicted by overgrooming in response to stress	Take to the vet
Hair loss and scaly skin Not itchy	Ringworm (fungal infection) (see photograph p115)	Take to the vet
Scratching, skin red, appears wet, on back of neck or inner thighs	Eosinophilic granuloma complex	Take to the vet
Scratching, excessive licking, may be skin change	Allergy to fleas, food or environment (or mites e.g. Demodex or Notoedres)	If flea control is adequate, take to vet. Or treat for fleas (see pp110–111)
Scratching, chewing, pussy and inflamed skin, may be bleeding	Pyoderma (deep bacterial infection)	Take to the vet
Ulcer on lip or nose	Eosinophilic granuloma complex	Take to the vet
Lump or swelling within the skin Not painful	Lipoma (fatty tumor) hematoma (blood blister), skin tumor, sebaceous cyst	Take to the vet in each case
Lump or swelling within the skin, painful, may be discharging fluid	Abscess	Take to the vet

STOMACH PROBLEMS

SIGNS	SOME POSSIBLE CAUSES	ACTION
Vomiting, longhaired cat	Fur ball	Talk to vet about diet, laxatives or oil Comb more often

SIGNS	SOME POSSIBLE CAUSES	ACTION
Eating grass, then vomiting grass and mucus Hair or prey remains may be included in vomitus	Natural evacuation of indigestible material	Carry out protocol for vomiting (see p147)
As above, fluid only	Mild gastritis	Carry out protocol for vomiting
Vomiting frequently, refusing food, depressed.	Gastritis Pancreatitis Obstruction (possibly a fur ball)	Take to the vet in each case
As above, plus diarrhea (with or without blood), dark tarry feces	Feline infectious enteritis (FIE) Feline leukemia virus (FeLV) Poisoning	Take to the vet in each case
As above, plus hunched posture	Foreign body lodged in stomach Pancreatitis	Take to the vet, urgent action required
Distended abdomen, young cat, may be lethargic, poor coat	Worm burden	Treat for worms (see pp112-115)

URINARY PROBLEMS

SIGNS	SOME POSSIBLE CAUSES	ACTION
Excessive thirst, bad breath, large quantities of urine, mouth ulcers, weight loss, anemia, vomiting	Chronic kidney disease (nephritis) resulting from an infection, chronic degeneration, tumor or inherited defect	Measure cat's water intake over a day Take this information to the vet
Young animal, failing to thrive, excessive thirst, very pale urine	Juvenile renal disease (inherited)	Take to the vet
Smelly urine, may contain blood, frequent urination or urine leaking, may be licking vulva or penis	Cystitis (inflammation of bladder) due to infection, bladder stones or stress	Take to the vet
Male cat, straining to pass urine, may be vomiting and yowling	Urethral blockage, possibly by a bladder stone	URGENT ACTION REQUIRED Take to the vet immediately

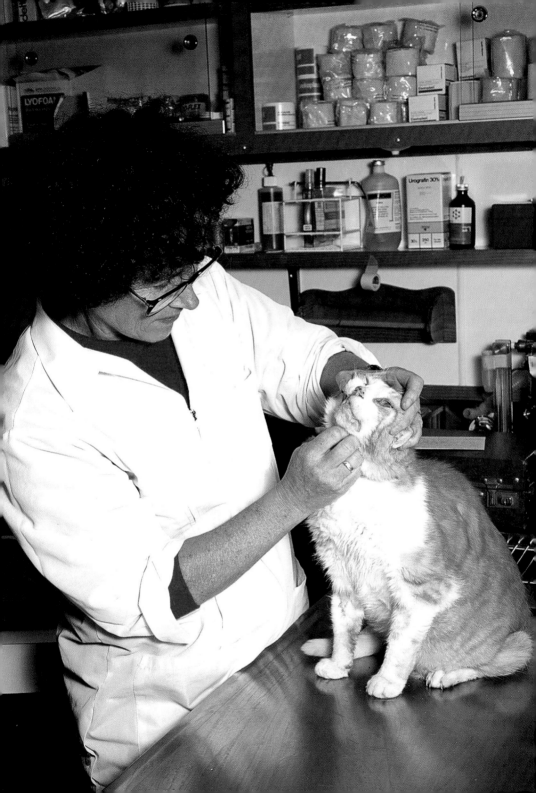

10. FIRST AID

▶ EMERGENCY TREATMENT ◀

The information given below is for guidance only, and is not intended to replace veterinary advice. If faced with an emergency, remember that the principles of first aid for cats are similar to those for humans.

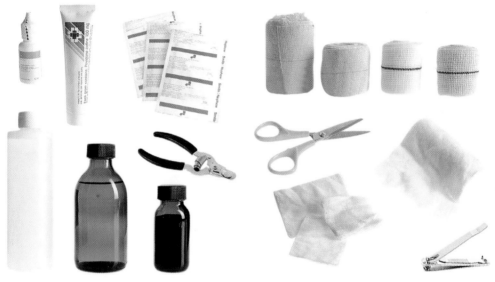

A BASIC FIRST-AID KIT

- several rolls of 1 inch and 2 inch bandages
- self-adhesive bandages
- 1 inch crepe bandage
- a roll of 2 inch by 3 inch adhesive bandage
- non-stick gauze pads
- cotton balls
- tweezers
- curved, blunt-ended scissors
- straight scissors
- nail clippers
- antiseptic and disinfectant liquids
- a tube of antiseptic cream
- hydrogen peroxide (3 per cent) for flushing wounds
- medicinal paraffin for the treatment of constipation
- a product to induce vomiting (ask your vet to recommend a substance and dosage)
- ear and eye drops as recommended by your veterinarian
- a roll of absorbent paper towel

Opposite: *Once your cat is 10 years old or so, it should get a thorough veterinary check-up every year.*

▶ MINOR WOUNDS ◀

A cat's natural instinct is to lick and clean up any wounds it suffers. A wound exposed to the air will usually dry up and heal more quickly.

Where minor wounds are involved, you can usually clip off the surrounding hair and then check for and remove thorns, glass, or other embedded objects. Flush the wound with saline or three per cent hydrogen peroxide, then leave the cat to look after itself. Do keep an eye on any minor wound, though, because if the licking becomes excessive the cat may cause skin changes and introduce infection – if this happens, ask your veterinarian for advice.

It is often difficult for an owner to bandage an affected area, and in many cases a cat will remove a bandage soon after it has been applied.

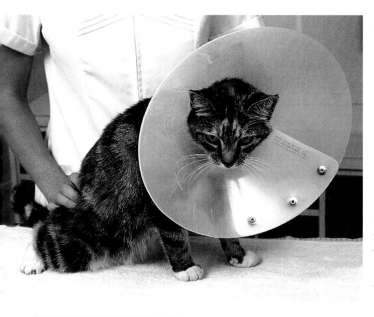

Adhesive tape can be applied over a bandage to reduce this risk, but it should be done by a veterinary nurse or a veterinarian. Your vet may recommend an (see left) collar as a last resort to prevent a cat from licking at a wound.

If the wound is on a part of the cat's body that it cannot reach, clip off the hair around the wound and flush it with a saline solution (made up of two tablespoons of salt in two cups of water), or three per cent hydrogen peroxide, or an antiseptic solution recommended by your vet.

▶ BITE WOUNDS AND PUNCTURE WOUNDS ◀

Some of these may appear minor, but by their nature they have the potential to cause problems. The opening will heal over very quickly, and any infection that has been introduced (as is often the case) will be trapped inside and may form an abscess.

The cat may lick the puncture wound and keep it open, or you can do the same by frequent bathing with saline. If you are in any doubt about what to do, or if the wound appears infected, get veterinary advice, because antibiotic treatment is usually necessary.

Top: *Elizabethan collars may be used to prevent cats from licking a wound or lesion on the body, or damaging surgical sites on the ears or eyes. Cats should not be allowed to go outside while wearing these collars.*

▶ BLEEDING FROM A VEIN ◀

If your cat is bleeding from a vein, the blood will be seeping out and dark in color. Try to flush the wound with saline or three per cent strength of hydrogen peroxide.

If the wound is on a limb, try to apply a pressure bandage as follows:

○ Cover the wound with a non-stick gauze pad.

○ Place a thick pad of damp cotton wool over the top.

○ Bandage firmly (but not tightly). Use good-quality bandages and keep the tightness even.

○ Check at regular intervals to make sure that there is no swelling below the wound (a sign that the bandage is too tight).

○ You could bandage the limb all the way to the foot and envelop the foot, to prevent this type of swelling.

○ Arrange for a veterinary check.

If the wound is on an area that you cannot bandage, apply the non-stick pad and cotton wool, then use your thumb or fingers to apply gentle pressure for up to five minutes at a time. If bleeding continues, get help as soon as you can.

▶ BLEEDING FROM AN ARTERY ◀

Arterial blood is bright red and spurts out with the force of the pumping heart.

○ If the blood vessel or artery involved is not too large, apply a pressure bandage as above and check every 10 minutes to make sure that bleeding has stopped.

○ For larger blood vessels and arteries, use your fingers to apply firm pressure over the affected area, but slightly closer to the heart. Release pressure after five minutes, then re-apply if necessary.

○ As soon as possible, take the cat to a vet.

Top: *Care should be taken when applying bandages. If they are too tight, they may restrict the blood flow. Cats can be difficult to bandage when conscious, especially if in pain – this cat is under sedation.*

▶ BLEEDING FROM A NAIL ◀

Bleeding from a nail is usually associated with an accident, and in most cases the nail will have been torn off completely. The wound will usually be very painful and the cat probably will not allow you to touch it. If the cat does allow you to touch it, protect the wound by placing a sterile pad over the injured area, and then wrap a bandage around the whole paw. Blood clotting should occur within five minutes, but the wound will need further treatment and antibiotic protection, so contact your veterinary clinic as soon as possible.

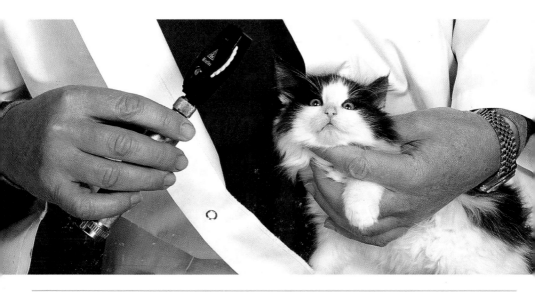

▶ EYE INJURIES ◀

You can deal with minor problems such as dust or dirt in the eye by flushing the eye with the eye drops kept in your first-aid kit, or, in an emergency, an eye solution for humans.

Remember though, that the surface of the eye (cornea) is very fragile and damage to it may not become evident for several days. For this reason, keep a close watch on any eye problem and get it checked out by a vet if you are in any doubt.

▶ EAR INJURIES ◀

Ear injuries may result from a catfight, or the cat's ear catching on an obstruction such as a twig. Surface veins on the ear are easily damaged and bleeding may occur. Unless the wound is obviously minor, it is best to get a veterinary surgeon to check it over.

Top: *This vet is using an ophthalmoscope to check a kitten's eyes for injuries.*

▶ MOUTH INJURIES ◀

These are usually caused by a sharp bone. Minor wounds to tongue or gums will usually heal without incident, but if you are in any doubt, get a veterinary check-up.

To remove a fish hook caught in a cat's lip, try to push the barb all the way through, then cut the hook through its shank. If you can't do this yourself, get veterinary help.

▶ LEG AND PAW INJURIES ◀

Superficial wounds on the lower leg can be flushed with saline, then dressed, bandaged, and protected by an old sock. Deeper ones need medical attention. Cuts on a footpad are more difficult to treat; unless minor they are best left to a veterinarian for assessment.

▶ TAIL INJURIES ◀

Cats are not always careful about keeping their tails from under human feet, but more usually, wounds are caused during fighting. Treat as described above (leg and paw injuries). If there is severe pain around the affected area, the tail may be fractured, so get veterinary advice.

Sometimes the tail gets trapped under a vehicle tire, and in trying to run away the cat pulls the tail violently, causing severe damage to the nerves. In many cases of nerve damage, the tail can be paralyzed – the damage is permanent and the only treatment is tail amputation.

▶ FRACTURES ◀

If a leg is fractured, restrict the cat's movement as much as possible. You can provide support to an injured lower limb by tying a newspaper or magazine around it. If in doubt, leave it alone or you could aggravate the existing damage. Get professional help.

For first aid to fractured ribs, use any materials you can find to wrap around the whole chest. Take the cat to a vet.

Above: *Radiography is only one of the many diagnostic procedures available to veterinary surgeons.*

► ACCIDENTS AND EMERGENCIES ◄

Before you begin any emergency treatment, you will need to check for the cat's heartbeat. Place two fingers over the lower center of the chest, just behind the elbow of the front leg, and press down lightly. Do not move the cat unless it is in danger (for example, lying in the street).

ARTIFICIAL RESPIRATION (AR)

- Remove the cat's collar and wipe away any saliva, blood, or vomit. Pull the tongue forward (use a handkerchief for better grip).
- Place the cat on its side.
- Place one hand over the cat's mouth to keep it closed.
- Take a deep breath and blow strongly into the cat's nostrils for about three seconds until you feel resistance or see the chest rise.
- Repeat this procedure 12–15 times over one minute.
- Stop, and watch the chest to see if the cat is breathing on its own.
- If the cat is not breathing, continue to perform the above procedure.
- Get veterinary help as soon as possible.

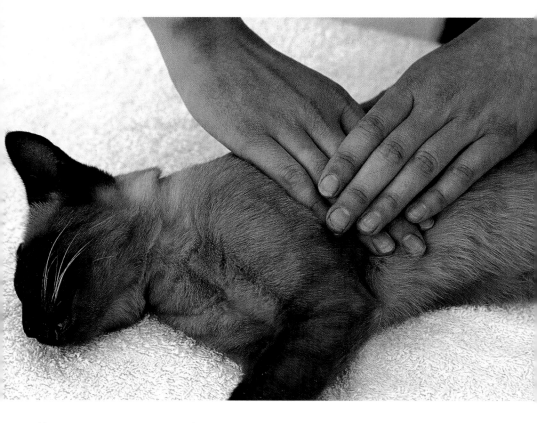

Above: *Do not attempt CPR unless it is impossible to get to a vet, as you may cause severe damage by performing this procedure incorrectly.*

CARDIOPULMONARY RESUSCITATION (CPR)

As with AR, this can be difficult to administer because the cat's body is so small.

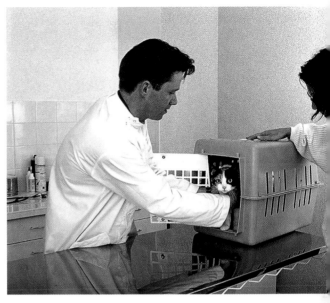

- Place the cat on its right side.
- Spread the fingers and the palm of one hand over the cat's chest.
- Apply smooth, rhythmical compressions that will move the chest about half an inch but not cause internal injury. Press once a second for half a minute.
- Stop, check for heartbeat (see opposite page, top – Accidents and emergencies).
- If there is no response, repeat the CPR procedure for another half a minute, then perform artificial respiration (see opposite page) for about one minute.
- Stop, and check for heartbeat and breathing.
- If neither is present, continue.
- If heartbeat only is present, continue AR.
- Get veterinary help as soon as possible.

ROAD TRAFFIC ACCIDENTS

- If the cat is on the street, get somebody to warn or control approaching traffic.
- Carefully slide the cat onto a piece of cloth, clothing, or something similar and move it off the road to a safe area.
- Check for heartbeat and breathing.
- If the cat has a heartbeat, but is not breathing, perform artificial respiration (see opposite page).
- If the heart is not beating, perform CPR (see above).
- An injured cat that is conscious will be frightened, aggressive, or both. Act and move as calmly and quietly as possible, all the time talking to, and reassuring the cat.
- Use the cloth or clothing to load the cat into a vehicle for transportation to a veterinary clinic. Excessive handling could exacerbate some injuries, especially spinal fractures.
- If you think there is a spinal injury, and you have the materials on hand, slide the cat onto a solid board and tie it down to restrict its movement.
- If the only way you can move the cat is to pick it up, do so very carefully using one hand in front of the chest and the other under its rump, keeping its spine as straight and as still as possible.

Top: *It is sensible to take your cat to the vet in a box or carrier. This helps it to feel secure and removes the risk of the cat escaping from your arms when frightened by a dog in the waiting room, or the sound of a passing car on the street.*

▶ SHOCK ◀

Accident victims suffer shock. Signs are:
- rapid breathing
- pale or white gums
- rapid heartbeat.

WHAT TO DO

- If the cat is unconscious, lay it on its side and pull its tongue out to keep its airway open, then place something under the cat's hips to raise its hindquarters.
- If the cat is conscious, try to calm it.
- Try to stop any visible bleeding (see p135).
- Keep the cat warm, but do not apply heat.
- Get veterinary help as soon as possible.

▶ ELECTRICAL SHOCK ◀

- If the affected cat is still in contact with the electrical source, SWITCH OFF THE POWER before you touch the cat.
- Check the cat for heartbeat and breathing (see Accidents and emergencies p138).
- If there is a pulse but no breathing, try to perform artificial respiration (see AR p138).
- If the heart is not beating, try cardiopulmonary resuscitation (see CPR p139).
- Get the cat to a vet as soon as possible.

▶ DROWNING ◀

- If you can, hold the cat upside down by its back legs and swing it from side to side for 15–20 seconds to help the water drain out of its lungs.
- Lay the cat on its side, sloping with its head down.
- Check for a heartbeat and breathing.
- If there is a heartbeat but no breathing, try to perform artificial respiration (see p138).
- If there is no heartbeat, try to perform CPR (see p139).
- Get the cat to a vet as soon as possible.

▶ CARBON MONOXIDE, SMOKE OR OTHER VAPOR INHALATION ◀

- Carry the cat into fresh air.
- If this is not possible, open windows, ventilate the area, and ensure that the cat is in a position where it can breathe fresh air, for instance next to an open window.
- If the cat is conscious, flush out the eyes with clean water.
- If the cat is unconscious, check its heartbeat and ascertain whether it is still breathing.
- If the heart is beating but there is no breathing, try to perform artificial respiration (see p138).
- If you cannot detect the cat's heartbeat, try to carry out cardiopulmonary resuscitation – CPR (see p139).
- Get the cat to a vet as soon as possible.

▶ CHOKING ◀

○ If possible, get help to restrain the cat.
○ Use the fingers and thumb of one hand to press the upper lips over the teeth in the upper jaw. Further firm pressure will force the mouth open.
○ If you can see the object that is causing choking, try to remove it, but be careful that you don't get bitten.
○ If removal this way is not possible and the cat is quite small, hold it by its hind legs, head down, and shake it vigorously.
○ Get the cat to a vet as soon as possible.

▶ CONVULSIONS OR FITS ◀

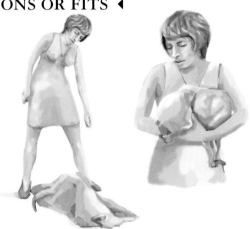

These usually last for only a few minutes, and are rarely fatal. Your objectives are to prevent the cat from injuring itself while convulsing, and avoid injury yourself.

○ Keep your fingers away from the cat's mouth.
○ Move it to a clear area, away from furniture and other obstacles.
○ Lightly wrap the cat in a blanket to help restrain its body movements. The darkness may also calm it.
○ Contact your veterinarian for advice.

▶ BURNS ◀

Burns may be caused by heat, or by chemicals such as petroleum products, strong acids, or alkalis.

BURNS CAUSED BY HEAT

○ Get the cat to a veterinarian as soon as possible.
○ While doing so, apply cold water or an ice pack (for example, a clean package of frozen vegetables) to the affected area.
○ Try to prevent the cat from licking the area.
○ If the burns are extensive, cover the affected area with a sterile, non-stick dressing.

BURNS CAUSED BY CHEMICALS

○ Thoroughly wash the area affected with soap and water (preferably use a soap that is mild, unscented, and uncolored).
○ Try to determine the cause.
○ Get veterinary advice (conveying the details if you have discovered the cause).

Top: *The best procedure when your cat has convulsions is to throw a towel or light blanket over it. When you need to calm down a nervous or distressed cat it also often works to cover it with a light blanket.*

▶ HEAT STROKE ◀

Signs include rapid, irregular breathing, panting, vomiting, and collapse.
- Get the cat into a cool environment.
- If the cat is unconscious, apply artificial respiration and/or cardiopulmonary resuscitation as necessary (see p138–139).
- Use a garden hose or a bath of cold water to cool the cat for up to half an hour. It is also a good idea to place an ice pack (for example, a clean packet of frozen vegetables) on the cat's head.
- Get veterinary help.

▶ HYPOTHERMIA ◀

- Warm the cat using an electric blanket or similar heating pad, turning the cat every few minutes.
- Otherwise, use a warm water bottle covered in a cloth. Do not exceed 100°F.
- Get veterinary help.

▶ FROSTBITE ◀

The areas most commonly affected by frostbite on a cat are those with little hair or a minimal blood supply, such as the tips of the ears and the nose.
- Apply a towel or similar material soaked in warm water. In order to avoid burning the cat, ensure that the compress is no hotter than 75°F.
- Check the skin color. If it appears dark, get veterinary help immediately.

▶ INSECT STINGS AND SPIDER BITES ◀

A great variety of insects and spiders are poisonous. Just as in humans, stings or bites may produce an allergic reaction.
- If the sting is from a bee, use a blunt knife to scrape off the stinger embedded in the skin. Do not simply try to pull it out.
- Apply ice to the affected area.
- Get veterinary help as soon as possible.

▶ POISONOUS TOADS AND LIZARDS ◀

The Blue-tailed Lizard and at least nine species of toad are capable of poisoning cats. If a cat licks or bites a toad, a toxin (carried in the wart-like lumps on the toad's skin) enters the cat's mouth and (often) its eyes. If it eats the tail of a Blue-tailed Lizard, it ingests the poison contained in it. Clinical signs appear soon after the incident, and include salivation, vomiting, shaking or trembling, lack of coordination, convulsions, and coma.
- If possible, immediately flush out the cat's mouth and eyes with water.
- If it is unconscious, wrap it in a blanket to keep it warm.
- In all cases take it to your vet for emergency treatment.

▶ SNAKE BITES ◀

Both venomous and non-venomous snakes can bite. However, venomous snakes leave a distinctly different imprint from that left by a non-venomous species, but these are difficult to see under a cat's fur. If you are not sure about the bite's origin, treat it as if it were poisonous. If you can handle the cat, try to stop lymphatic spread – bandage firmly, splint, and immobilize.

The lymphatic system is responsible for systemic spread of most venoms. This can be reduced by the application of a firm bandage (as firm as you would put on a sprained ankle) over a folded pad placed over the bitten area. While firm, it should not be so tight that it stops blood flow to the limb or congests the veins. Start bandaging directly over the bitten area, ensuring that the pressure over the bite is firm and even. If you have enough bandage you can extend towards more central parts of the body to delay spread of any venom that has already started to move centrally. A pressure dressing should be applied even if the bite is on the victim's trunk or torso.

Immobility is best attained by application of a splint or sling, using anything at hand to minimize all limb movement.

The pressure-immobilization approach is simple, safe, and will not cause tissue damage (i.e. from incision, injection, freezing, or arterial tourniquets – all of which are ineffective). Do not cut or excise the area or apply an arterial tourniquet! Both these measures are ineffective and may make the situation worse.

Bites to the head, neck, and back are a special problem – firm pressure should be applied locally if possible.

Removal of the bandage will result in rapid systemic spread. Therefore, wait until the cat is in a fully-equipped medical treatment area before bandage removal is attempted.

▶ AN ENCOUNTER WITH A SKUNK ◀

Skunks are one of the major carriers of rabies and should not be handled with bare hands. Follow these procedures if your cat has encountered a skunk and been sprayed over the face or body.

- O Restrain the cat
- O Flush its eyes with clean water
- O Wash and rinse its body thoroughly with soap and water

- O To neutralize the odor, use a skunk odor neutralizer, or liberally apply plain tomato juice from the kitchen
- O If the skunk has died, DO NOT HANDLE IT WITH YOUR BARE HANDS. Take the carcass to a veterinarian to establish if the animal was rabid.
- O Ensure that your cat is vaccinated against rabies and given appropriate boosters.

Top: *Preventing the spread of poison from a snakebite is the essence of treatment.*

▶ POISONOUS SUBSTANCES IN AND AROUND THE HOME ◀

Safety around the home is just as important for pets as it is for small children.

A liquid or powder that has leaked or been spilled from a container can get onto a cat's fur or paw pads and, in cleaning this off, the cat is likely to ingest the toxic substance. You may find that your cat develops a real liking for the taste of bleach (the scented bleaches are more likely to appeal) and some cats will even lick it off wiped surfaces. All potentially poisonous substances should therefore be locked away, or stored safely out of a cat's reach, and where a cat or other animal cannot knock them down. Substances that can give off harmful vapors should be used and stored where there is adequate ventilation.

SYMPTOMS OF POISONING

Symptoms will vary, depending on what toxic substance is involved, and can be similar to those of many other medical conditions. However, you should consider the possibility of poisoning if your cat is:

O panting very heavily
O suddenly vomiting and/or has severe diarrhea (more than two or three times within an hour)
O drooling or foaming at the mouth
O crying
O suffering intense abdominal pain
O showing signs of shock
O depressed
O trembling, uncoordinated, staggering, or having convulsions
O collapsed or in a coma
O showing signs of an allergic reaction, such as swelling around the face or a red rash (hives) on the belly.

What to do:
O Time is critical
O Try to identify the poison
O Carry out the recommended emergency treatment described on p145
O Contact your veterinarian immediately and take your cat to the clinic
O If you have found the cat with a poisonous or unidentified substance, take the container or packet with you. The label should contain information about the antidote and treatment for that particular type of poisoning, which will reduce further delay

O If your cat has vomited, collect a specimen of the vomit in a clean container and take that with you.

EMERGENCY TREATMENT

If the poison is corrosive (strong acid or alkali) or petroleum-based (*see p146*), or if you are not sure what caused the problem:

○ DO NOT INDUCE VOMITING
○ If the cat is conscious, flush the mouth and muzzle with large quantities of water, then try to give one teaspoon of egg white or olive oil
○ Take the cat to your vet.

If the substance is not corrosive (*see p146*) nor petroleum-based:

○ If the cat has not already vomited, try to induce vomiting

○ Put the vomit material into a clean container
○ Take the cat and vomit material to the veterinarian.

TO INDUCE VOMITING

Give ONE of the following:

○ one large crystal of sodium carbonate straight down the throat
○ one heaped teaspoon of table salt in a little warm water
○ one tablespoon of mustard powder in a cup of warm water.

Repeat every 10 minutes until the cat vomits. Save the vomit for veterinary examination.

Below: *Cats wandering through overgrown garden areas may risk snakebites or encounters with other poisonous creatures. They may also come across poisonous plants or even hazardous material discarded by irresponsible neighbors.*

▶ SOME POTENTIAL SOURCES OF POISON ◀

Many of the plants in our yards and gardens, and the substances that we commonly use in the house, garden, garage, or shed, and don't always think of as 'poison', can be poisonous to cats and other pets (as well as small children, of course). Kittens are particularly at risk.

INSIDE YOUR HOME

PETROLEUM PRODUCTS
O Dry-cleaning solution

CORROSIVE PRODUCTS
O Detergents in concentrated form, such as those for use in dishwashers or automatic washing machines, dry-powder carpet cleaners
O Household bleaches (hypochlorites, chlorox)
O Disinfectants in concentrated form
O Corn and callous remover.

NON-CORROSIVE PRODUCTS
O Medicines (human or animal). Symptoms include vomiting, panting, acetone odor to breath, general weakness or collapse
O Many common indoor house plants are poisonous if eaten, such as poinsettia leaves and mistletoe.

O Cleaning agents and dry shampoos containing carbon tetrachloride
O Cleaning agents or solvents such as acetone or benzene
O Chocolate. It contains theobromine, a compound with a similar action to caffeine. It is a stimulant and irritant, and affects every organ of the body. The darker the chocolate, the more theobromine it contains. The amount of theobromine in chocolate intended for human consumption is safe for a human, but can harm a pet animal. Symptoms include digestive upset (diarrhea and vomiting), increased heartbeat and blood pressure, increased urine production causing excessive thirst, muscle twitching and convulsions. There is no known antidote.
Note: Pet chocolate drops are safe because the theobromine has been removed
O Carbon monoxide from leaking gas appliances, or improperly ventilated oil or solid fuel stoves. It is odorless, colorless and tasteless and therefore undetectable
O Smoke (from cigarettes, cigars, or open fires)

IN THE GARAGE OR SHED
PETROLEUM PRODUCTS
O Solvents and paint removers
O Engine oil

CORROSIVE SUBSTANCES
O Battery acid
O Grease remover
O Strong alkalis such as lye and other drain cleaners
O Creosote and tar

EMERGENCY ANTIDOTES
O Absorbents (to absorb toxic substances): activated charcoal, up to six 300 mg tablets, or two to three tablespoons of powder mixed in a cup of warm water
O Protectants (to help cover the stomach lining): one tablespoon of egg white or olive oil
O Against acids: one teaspoon of bicarbonate of soda
O Against alkalis: several teaspoons of vinegar or lemon juice

---

NON-CORROSIVE

O Plant and garden sprays and weed killers (fungicides and herbicides)

O Metaldehyde. Commonly used in slug and snail baits. Although many of these products contain a repellent to reduce the risk to cats, cases of cumulative poisoning do occur. A cat may ingest only a few baits at a time, but over a period enough metaldehyde can accumulate inside its body to cause poisoning. Metaldehyde may also be present in the compressed tablets used to fuel small heaters

O Antifreeze (ethylene glycol). Some cats, especially kittens, tend to like the taste of antifreeze and will lap it if they discover it. It is extremely toxic and causes kidney damage. A tiny amount can be fatal. Symptoms usually begin an hour or two after ingestion

O Rat and mouse poisons. There are many different products. Active ingredients include arsenic, thallium, and warfarin

O Insecticides, especially pyrophosphates such as malathion. Potentially lethal. Absorption can occur through the skin

VAPORS

O Fumes from wood preserver, or acetone-based paint removers and solvents

IN THE GARDEN

O Mushrooms and fungi

O Berries

O Any part of plants such as azalea, bird of paradise, crocus, delphinium, foxglove, irises, ivy, jasmine, laburnum, larkspur, laurel, lilies, lily-of-the-valley, oleander, privet, rhododendron, sweet pea, wisteria

O Certain vegetables: rhubarb leaves (raw or cooked), tomato vines

IN THE CAR

O Carbon monoxide from a faulty exhaust

IN THE NEIGHBORHOOD

Poisonous substances may also be found in public areas away from your home.

O Rat poisons, laid by rodent eradicators

O Other poisons, such as bird or rabbit carcasses baited with poison to eliminate vermin in woodlands or forests

O Food contaminated with Salmonella or *Clostridium botulinum* bacteria. Cats are usually very fussy about what they eat, but salmonellosis (food poisoning) can be fatal in young animals. Botulism affects the nervous system and causes partial or complete paralysis

---

A PROTOCOL FOR ASSESSING AND TREATING VOMITING

In cats, vomiting is a natural way of eliminating material from the stomach and does not necessarily indicate an emergency: it may simply be getting rid of indigestible material such as the remains of a prey victim. If your cat vomits once or twice, and otherwise appears bright, monitor its progress for a few hours. If no more vomiting occurs, offer it small amounts of food over the next 24 hours, and if all is well, reintroduce its normal diet.

You must consult your vet if you are in any doubt, or

O the cat appears depressed

O there is blood in the vomit

O the cat is vomiting intermittently (e.g. every three to four hours) for more than eight hours

O the cat is vomiting continuously

O the cat has had access to potentially poisonous substances.

11. BREED DIRECTORY

Originally, cat breeds were divided into two classes: Shorthairs and Longhairs, purely on the basis of coat length. However, the distinction between these classes became blurred as new breeds with quite different body conformations, such as the Siamese, were introduced from Asia. Also, new breeds were developed that combined various body characteristics and had semi-long coats, with the result that long-haired cats could be classified in the Shorthair class, and vice versa.

The classification of cat breeds is now usually done according to type, rather than length of hair. Type summarizes the body characteristics of the cat, such as head and ear shape, body and tail length, leanness or stockiness. It has nothing to do with color and very little to do with coat length. The Oriental and Foreign class, for instance, includes breeds developed in Europe and America, but that still reflect the longer and leaner body shape (type) typical of the Siamese.

▶ COLORS AND PATTERNS ◀

The cat's original coat was of agouti hair (each hair is ticked along its length with dark and light bands of a basic color), designed for camouflage. The first mutation to a solid color was probably black. Blue is a dilute of Black, Cream is a dilute of Red, while Lilac and Lavender are dilutes of Chocolate. The basic colors have different names in different parts of the world. Some of them are: Black (Ebony), Blue, Chocolate (Havana Brown), Sorrel, Cinnamon, Lilac, Lavender, Red, Cream, White, Silver.

Colors can occur singly or in various combinations produced by different genes. There are several recognized patterns.

'Self' and 'solid' refer to a coat that is all one color and of uniform shade from root to tip.

Himalayan, or pointed, pattern refers to the gene that removes color from most of the body, but not the extremities – feet, tail, ears, and face – resulting in a pale body with contrasting colored 'points'. The best known example of this pattern is the Siamese.

The tabby is the 'wild' coat pattern, which consists of clearly defined colored markings on a colored ground, usually a wavy or striped pattern on gray and brown. It can appear in various colors, but the most commonly seen is the orange (ginger).

The patched, or broken-colored pattern can consist of two or three colors. This group also includes the tortoiseshells (torties), with their black, cream, and brownish markings. The combination of tortoiseshell and white is known as calico. Smoke refers to a coat pattern created when the guard hairs have colored tips, while the undercoat is pale.

A coat is called shaded when the color shades gradually down the sides, face, and tail, being darkest on the top of the head and lightest under the belly and tail.

Opposite: *An Oriental Red showing tabby markings, and the long legs of the Siamese type.*

▶ ABYSSINIAN ◀

According to legend the Abyssinian is descended from an ancient Egyptian breed, but its actual origins are obscure. Some people suggest that the present line originated from an import into Britain from Abyssinia (now Ethiopia) in 1868, which in fact looked nothing like today's breed. Others argue that the breed was created much later. Whatever the true facts, the 'Abby' has many admirers.

The Abyssinian and its long-haired version, the Somali, are unique among cat breeds in that they carry the mutant Abyssinian gene *Ta* (one of the Tabby series), which produces their characteristic ticked coat. This color was known by several different names, including Rabbit, Bunny, or Hare, because of the resemblance in color pattern. The French still refer to the normal Abyssinian coloring as *lièvre*, or hare.

PHYSICAL CHARACTERISTICS

The Abyssinian cat is a 'foreign' type, of medium build – firm, lithe, and muscular, but never large or coarse. It is often described as having an alert, wild look. The head is broad and tapering to show a modified, slightly rounded wedge without flat planes, set on an elegant neck. The brow, cheeks, and profile lines should show a gentle contour, with a slight nose break leading to a firm chin. The muzzle should not be

Above: *The coat of the Abyssinian Blue is a dilute of more traditional Ruddy.*

Above: *Fawn is the dilute version of Sorrel and was once called Cream.*

sharply pointed, rather it should form a narrow indentation. The ears should be set wide apart and pricked, broad at the base, comparatively large, well-cupped and preferably tufted. The eyes should be large, bright, and expressive, set well apart and colored amber, hazel or green. The body should be of medium length with a tail that is broad at the base, fairly long and tapering. The legs should be long, slender, and fine-boned, the feet small and oval.

The coat should be short, fine, soft, and close-lying, with double or preferably treble ticking (two to three bands of color on each hair). The darker hair color should extend well up the back of the hind legs and also show as a solid tip at the extreme end of the tail. A line of dark pigmentation is required around the eyes. Bars on the chest, legs, and tail are undesirable, and an unbroken necklet is not permissible. The Abyssinian cat has a tendency to whiteness in the immediate area of the lips and jaw, but this should not extend to the neck. A locket and other white markings are not permissible.

FAULTS (FEATURES FOR WHICH A CAT OF THIS BREED WOULD BE PENALIZED AT A SHOW)
Squint. Absence of correct dark markings and pigmentation.

TEMPERAMENT
The Abyssinian is alert, active, good-natured, intelligent, and full of curiosity. It makes a gentle household companion, but may be suspicious of strangers.

Above: *The ears should curve at least 90° in a smooth arc.*

This is simply an American household cat with a single, striking mutation: its ears curl away from the face towards the back and center of the head.

They originated in 1981 when a stray kitten with this mutation appeared at the home of Grace and Joe Ruga in Lakeland, California. An affectionate black female, she had a long, silky coat and they named her Shulamith, after the peaceful, `black and comely' princess of the Song of Songs in the Hebrew Bible. Shulamith had a litter of four kittens, two of which had the same curly ears. These cats were shown in California in 1983.

They are now fully recognized in North America. The first Curls to reach Europe arrived in Britain in 1995. Spontaneous mutations such as this can carry crippling side effects, however. Although none are apparent in the Curl, some registries fear that problems may yet arise.

All American curls are born with straight ears. When they are two to ten days old, the tips begin to curve. They then curl and uncurl until they 'set' permanently at about four months.

PHYSICAL CHARACTERISTICS
The ears curve at least 90° in a smooth arc. The head is a modified wedge with gentle curves. The eyes are walnut-shaped and slightly tilted. The body is moderately muscled and semi-foreign in shape.

TEMPERAMENT
Quietly affable.

▸ ANGORA ◂

The Angora was developed in Britain in the mid-1960s by mating a Sorrel Abyssinian to a Seal Point Siamese, in an attempt to produce a Siamese with ticked points. The descendants inherited the color trait, resulting in cinnamon Oriental Shorthairs. But they also inherited the gene for long hair, which resulted in the Angora. The breed is not related to the 19th century Angora, nor the revived Turkish Angora nor the recently created Oriental Longhair. In an attempt to avoid confusion, it is called the Javanese in Europe, but some North American associations use Javanese for some colors of Balinese. In a further attempt to avoid confusion, but really making it worse, the British Angora has been called the Oriental Longhair in North America.

PHYSICAL CHARACTERISTICS
Similar in type to the Oriental breeds, these animals have a body that is long and lean, culminating in a tail with an elegant plume. The tail is long, tapering to a fine end. The fine, silky, medium-length, coat lies flat on the body and has no woolly undercoat, making the cat fairly easy to groom.

The head is a moderate triangular wedge, with a fine muzzle, on a long, slender neck. The ears are large, with a wide base, and they follow the lines of the wedge.

The eyes are slanted and green in all colors of Angora, except White. The White must have blue eyes that are bright and vivid, rather than a pale, baby-blue.

The body is medium in size, svelte and muscular, the legs long, slim and well muscled, ending in small, oval paws. The hind legs are longer than the forelegs.

TEMPERAMENT
Similar in temperament to the Oriental breeds, these animals are lively, inquisitive, and energetic exhibitionists.

Above: *All Angoras except white, must have green eyes. The coat of this cat is Blue Spotted.*

Above: *The Balinese Lilac Lynx Point, a dilute version of Chocolate Point, can be a study in delicacy.*

This breed was developed in the United States during the 1940s from Siamese bloodlines that carried the recessive gene for long hair. The resultant long-haired Siamese were called Balinese because their appearance and movement reminded an early breeder of dancers on the Indonesian island of Bali. The Cat Fancy Association of America recognized the breed in 1970 in four point colors: Seal, Blue, Chocolate, and Lilac. In the 1980s additional colors were recognized under the name Javanese. In Britain all colors are recognized under the name Balinese. In New Zealand all self-colored and spotted forms of the Balinese are known as Javanese.

PHYSICAL CHARACTERISTICS
A semi-longhaired cat with well-proportioned head, body, legs, and tail. The facial expression should be one of alertness and intelligence. It is in effect a Siamese with long hair. The head is long and has a wedge shape. The width between the eyes tapers to a fine muzzle to form a straight profile. The chin is firm and in line with the upper jaw. The ears are wide at the base, large, and pointed. The typically Oriental eyes are almond-shaped, slanting towards the nose. In all varieties the color of the eyes must be a vivid, deep, sapphire blue.

The body is fine-boned, of medium size, it is lithe and svelte, with long tapering lines, but nevertheless strong and muscular. The legs are long and slim, the hind legs slightly longer than the forelegs. The feet are small and oval, the long, tapering tail is plumed.

The coat is long, fine and silky, close-lying and without a downy undercoat. The whole face is covered by a mask that is connected by tracings to the ears.

FAULTS (FEATURES FOR WHICH A CAT OF THIS BREED WOULD BE PENALIZED AT A SHOW)
Malocclusion of the teeth; white toe(s); deviation from the standard set for a particular color; incorrect eye color; permanent squint.

TEMPERAMENT
Similar to that of the Siamese, though less vocal. Active, intelligent, and affectionate, but somewhat demanding. The Balinese is sociable and usually gets on well with other cats, visitors, and dogs.

Still rare worldwide, this breed has a distinctively thick and luxurious coat. The first mating of an Asian leopard cat with a domestic cat in California in 1963 was accidental. Almost ten years later, Dr Willard Centrewall at the University of California continued this hybridization in order to examine the Asian leopard cat's resistance to feline leukemia virus (FeLV). The research was disappointing, but out of these beginnings appeared the Bengal. The first Bengal was registered in 1983. Initially this was a nervous feline family, but continued development has led to a more outgoing breed. Early crosses were to non-pedigrees, but as soon as the leopard-like coat appeared, individuals were crossed with an Indian street cat and Egyptian Maus.

PHYSICAL CHARACTERISTICS

The Bengal head is slightly longer than it is wide and the face has high cheekbones and a full, broad muzzle. The chin is strong, with widely set canine teeth helping to produce pronounced whisker pads. Frown lines and broken streaks cover the head, and the nose leather is pink, outlined in black. In profile, there is a gentle curve from forehead to nose, rather than a break. The ears are short, with a wide base and rounded tips, no tufts. The eyes are large, oval, and slightly slanted. The neck is thick and muscular. The body is large, very muscular and sleek, with a broad chest. The legs are strong and muscular and of medium length. The hind legs are longer than the forelegs and the paws are large and rounded.

TEMPERAMENT

Conservative. Because of the wildcat origins of the breed, a dependable temperament is a vital feature of breeding programs.

Above: *Slightly longer than it is wide, the Bengal's face has high cheekbones and pronounced whisker pads.*

Legend has it that this breed was sacred and appointed to guard the temples of Burma. A widely accepted ancestry is that a pregnant female was sent to France in 1919 and the resulting litter provided the foundation stock for the breed in Europe, Britain, and North America. However, some believe that they originated in France from the crossing of Siamese and Longhairs. Whatever the truth, the modern Birman displays the results of many generations of careful selective breeding. Like the Siamese and Balinese, it carries the Himalayan gene that causes the pointed pattern. The typical white 'gloves' on the front paws and 'gauntlets' on the hind feet may be due to a recessive white spotting gene. Although recognized in France in 1925, the breed did not gain recognition in Britain until 1966, with the United States following a year later.

PHYSICAL CHARACTERISTICS

A strong-boned semi-longhaired cat that does not conform to Persian type, but has a slightly longer head, neck, body, legs, and tail. There is strong definition at the border between the points and the white of the gloves and gauntlets.

The head is strongly boned and slightly rounded in the muzzle. The forehead is broader than high, slopes well back, and is slightly convex in profile with a flatter appearance in front of and between the ears. The jaws are strong, cheeks full and well developed. The nose is of medium length and the Australian and New Zealand standards require them to be slightly Roman in shape, with the nose pad set a little high. The chin should be full and strong with a straight bite. The ears should be of medium size, set moderately far apart and slightly

Above: *A Birman Red Point with charactersitic white gloves and gauntlets.*

Above: *The Birman Chocolate Point more closely resembles the original Seal Point coloring of the breed.*

adult should cover the face to above the eyes and be joined to the ears by tracings only, leaving the body color in front of the ears quite apparent. The chin is shaded to match the mask. The leg point color should extend to just above the elbows on the front legs. The inside of the legs should be of a lighter color. The front paws should be white-gloved, in an even line at the level of the third joint. The back paws have white gauntlets which cover the back paws and extend in line ('laces') up the back of the legs to a point, in the shape of a spear-head, just below the middle of the hock. Although the breeder's aim is to perfect the white feet, because this feature is the Birman's defining characteristic, they are not given preference over the 'type' of the cat. A cat may be slightly imperfect in its gloves and gauntlets, yet still eligible for awards.

flared, with rounded tips. The eyes are almost round, set well apart and colored a clear, sapphire blue – the deeper the better.

Males are much more robust than females. The legs are strong-boned and thick-set, of medium length, with large round paws. All varieties have pink paw pads. Birmans walk with a stiff rear-legged gait. The tail is of medium length (reaching to its shoulders), bushy, with the fur slightly oval at the tip, flowing in repose, but carried thrown backwards with a curl at the tip.

The coat is of medium length and has a silky texture. There is a full ruff round the neck, and the hair is slightly curled on the belly. The fur is of such a texture that it will not mat. The tail is bushy. The mask in the

FAULTS (FEATURES FOR WHICH A CAT OF THIS BREED WOULD BE PENALIZED AT A SHOW)
Squint. Strongly almond-shaped eyes. Areas of white in points other than gloves or gauntlets. Blotches or spots of color in gloves or gauntlets. Lack of width in the head; small, rounded ears; white chin.

TEMPERAMENT
Moderate and adaptable – somewhere between the placid Persians and the demanding Siamese. Gentle and affectionate, they get on well with other pets and visitors.

▸ BRITISH SHORTHAIR ◂

These are large, tough-looking cats. Because of their masculine appearance, 'Brits' are often preferred by men. Brought to the USA from Britain in the early 1900s, they were only recognized here as a breed in 1970 and then only in blue and black. The original members of this group were developed during the 19th century from ordinary short-haired domestic cats. At one stage, long-haired varieties were also included in breeding programs to improve the type. This resulted in today's breed which is a broad-chested, rather stocky animal with a relatively large head, short strong legs, and large round paws. It was one of the first breeds to be shown at the Crystal Palace in London, where the first 'benched' cat show was held in 1871.

The European Shorthair is much the same and has similar breed standards. By contrast the American Shorthair, which evolved in an environment with more natural predators, is larger and less stocky, with comparatively longer legs and tail, and a more oblong head.

PHYSICAL CHARACTERISTICS

A compact, well-balanced, powerful, and muscular cat with a relatively compact body and short legs. The head is round and set on a short, thick neck. There should be good width between the ears, which should be small and rounded at the tips. The round face should have full round cheeks and a strong, firm deep chin. The forehead should be rounded and lead to a short, broad, straight nose. The eyes must be large, round, well-opened, and set wide apart. The body is cobby, comparatively massive and low-slung, with a deep broad chest and short level back. The legs are short and strong, with rounded paws. The tail is thick and of medium

Above: *Blue is one of the earliest colors in British Shorthairs and remains popular.*

BREEDS

length, thicker at the base and rounded at the tip. The coat is short, dense and crisp. Ideally, the density should be such that the coat appears to 'break' as the cat moves.

Above: *British Shorthair Red showing the typical round face and full cheeks.*

FAULTS (FEATURES FOR WHICH A CAT OF THIS BREED WOULD BE PENALIZED AT A SHOW)

Any anatomical abnormalities or deformities such as umbilical hernia or a squint. Soft, over-long, or fluffy coat; fluffy tail; pronounced nose stop; weak chin; pronounced whisker pads; incorrect color or pattern.

TEMPERAMENT

Though tough-looking, these 'gentle giants' are affectionate and easy-going. They adjust well to other pets and children. Their build and weight makes them poor climbers and some are even afraid of heights. They are intelligent and even-tempered; not temperamental. They are moderately active and playful.

Right: *Chocolate Point was accepted in Britain for this breed in the 1990s.*

▶ BURMESE (AMERICAN) ◀

Above: *The American Burmese is richly colored and round-eyed.*

The North American Burmese differs from its European counterparts in that its standard emphasizes roundness, notably in the shape of the head. The extremely round 'contemporary' look dates from the 1970s, as does the Burmese head fault, an inherited deformity of the skull that is often lethal or requires euthanasia.

The Burmese breed started with Wong Mau, a brown female from Rangoon in Myanmar (formerly Burma), brought to the United States by US Navy psychiatrist Joseph Thompson in 1930. Wong Mau was mated with a Siamese, the most similar breed.

PHYSICAL CHARACTERISTICS
As late as the 1980s Sable was the only color universally accepted for this breed.

Other colors had occurred since early breeding programs, but were known within the Cat Fanciers Association as Mandalays. Today coat colors include Blue, Champagne and Platinum, which in other breeds would be Lilac or Lavender. The close-lying coat is short and fine, with a satin-like texture and a glossy shine.

The head is pleasantly rounded, with full cheeks, and the muzzle is short and broad, with a rounded chin. The eyes are round and have a golden color. The medium-sized ears have rounded tips, are widely spaced and tilt forward. The body is medium-sized, muscular and compact.

TEMPERAMENT
Friendly and relaxed.

▶ BURMESE (EUROPEAN) ◀

European breeders, followed by those in New Zealand, Australia, and South Africa, have opted for a well-muscled, but more angular shape in Burmese, as opposed to the rounded look on the American side of the Atlantic. The European Burmese is descended from the American breed. American cats were imported into Europe after World War II and the brown was recognized in 1952 by the Governing Council of the Cat Fancy (GCCF). However, the Europeans preferred the more Oriental look and were interested in a wider range of colors. A further change came in 1996 when the Fédération Internationale Féline (FIFé) amended its breed standard to allow green eyes. The long-haired variety of Burmese is known as the Tiffany in America, but in Britain the Tiffanie was developed from Burmilla and Burmese.

PHYSICAL CHARACTERISTICS
The more Oriental look requires a moderately wedge-shaped head, oval eyes, and long legs. The widely-set ears are medium-sized and rounded at the tip. The muzzle is blunt, with a deep chin. The hind legs are slightly longer than the forelegs. The paws are oval and the tail has a rounded tip. The coat is short and fine, lying close to the body.

TEMPERAMENT
Friendly and relaxed, it is ideally suited to life in active households.

Above: *In the Burmese, tortie patterns may be dramatically blotched. This is a Blue Tortie.*

▶ CORNISH REX ◀

In rexed cats, long and short-haired, hair growth is genetically retarded. The Cornish Rex has no guard hairs, while the Devon Rex has soft guard hairs, which are virtually identical to down hairs. The Cornish Rex's coat is soft to the touch, like cut velvet.

In 1950 a cat with a short, curly coat, completely lacking in guard hairs, was born to a farm cat in Cornwall. Its owner named it Kallibunker and later contacted a well-known cat breeder and a rabbit fancier who had an interest in genetics. Following a breeding program it was confirmed that the unusual coat was due to a mutant recessive gene. A similar gene causes the curly coat in the Rex rabbit, after whom the cat breed was named. In 1957 two of Kallibunker's descendants were sent to the United States and founded the breed here.

Originally all Rex cats were grouped together as one breed, but the Cornish Rex and Devon Rex were given separate recognition in Britain in 1967, in New Zealand in 1969, Australia in 1972, and in the United States in 1979. In Europe a cat with a similar coat was known as the German Rex. In Britain the German Rex was considered to be the same breed as the Cornish. However, the German Rex is more solidly built than the Cornish and conforms to the European Shorthair type, so the breeds were given separate status in 1982.

Above: *The red gene was present in the Cornish Rex from Kallibunker's own offspring.*

BREEDS

Above: *A White Cornish Rex showing the short, thick, plush coat without guard hairs.*

PHYSICAL CHARACTERISTICS

A fine-boned, elegant cat of modified foreign type. The head has a medium wedge, with a length about one third greater than the maximum width, narrowing to a strong chin. The skull is flat. In profile the line from the center of the forehead to the end of the nose should be straight. The eyes must be oval-shaped, medium in size, and of a color in keeping with the coat. The ears must be large, set rather high, wide at the base, and tapering to rounded tops. They should be well covered with fine fur. The body is hard and muscular, slender and of medium length. The legs are long and straight, giving the cat an overall appearance of being 'high on the legs.' The paws are small and oval. The tail is long, fine, and tapering, well covered with curly fur. The coat is short, thick, and plush, without guard hairs. It should curl, wave, or ripple, particularly on the back and tail. The whiskers and eyebrows are crinkled and of good length. All coat colors are acceptable. Any white markings must be symmetrical, except in the Tortoiseshell and White. Varieties with Siamese-type colored points are known as Si-Rex.

FAULTS (FEATURES FOR WHICH A CAT OF THIS BREED WOULD BE PENALIZED AT A SHOW)

Asymmetrical white markings, except in Tortoiseshell and White; shaggy or too short a coat; bare patches; British head type or too long a wedge; small ears; cobby body; lack of firm muscles; short or bare tail.

TEMPERAMENT

They are intelligent and affectionate. Playful and sociable cats that can be rather extroverted and quite vocal.

▶ DEVON REX ◀

Above: *Oversized, low-set ears and dramatic eyes give the Devon Rex an elfin appearance.*

In 1960 a curly coated feral cat was noticed near a disused tin mine in Devon. It later mated with another stray, which was being fed by a local resident. The stray produced a curly-coated kitten with a distinctive pixie-like head shape. The kitten was adopted and named Kirlee. At that time there had been a lot of publicity about the Cornish Rex, so Kirlee's owner made contact with the breeder who was conducting the Cornish Rex program.

However, when Kirlee was mated with a Cornish Rex, only normal-coated kittens were born. After several such matings it was realized that the gene causing Kirlee's coat was not the same as that producing the curly coat of the Cornish Rex. A second breeding program was set up to produce cats similar to Kirlee, with his unique head shape and a slightly more muscular body than the Cornish Rex. Because of their characteristic head shape, these cats are often referred to as Pixies.

PHYSICAL CHARACTERISTICS
An elegant cat with a unique head shape and a slender, but relatively muscular body. The head is wedge-shaped, with a full-cheeked face. The muzzle is short, with a strong chin and whisker break. The nose has a strongly marked stop. The forehead curves back to a flat skull. The eyes are wide-set, large, oval, and slope towards the outer edges of the ears. The eye-color should be in keeping with the coat color or (except in the Si-Rex) chartreuse (green-yellow), green or yellow. The ears are large, set rather low, very wide at the base, tapering to rounded tops, and well

Above: *The Devon Rex is never bored, as shown by the keen expression of this Seal Tortie.*

covered with fine fur. The body is hard and muscular, slender and of medium length, broad in the chest, carried high on long slim legs, with the length of the hind legs emphasized. The paws are small and oval. The neck is slender, the tail fine, long and tapering, and well covered with short fur. The coat is very short and fine, wavy, soft, and without guard hairs. The whiskers and eyebrows are crinkled, rather coarse, and of medium length. All coat colors are acceptable. Varieties with Siamese-type colored points are called Si-Rex.

FAULTS (FEATURES FOR WHICH A CAT OF THIS BREED WOULD BE PENALIZED AT A SHOW)

Straight or shaggy coat; bare patches; narrow, long, or British-type head; cobby body; lack of firm muscles; small or high-set ears; short, bare, or bushy tail.

Right: *This Black Devon Rex shows the slender neck and broad chest of the breed.*

TEMPERAMENT

In temperament these cats are similar to the Cornish Rex. They are intelligent and affectionate, playful and sociable, occasionally extrovert, and may be somewhat vocal.

▶ DOMESTIC SHORTHAIR ◀

Above: *The only breed standard for Domestic Shorthairs is probably `cute.'*

Even in countries with high populations of pedigree cats, the random-bred Domestic Shorthair outnumbers the pedigree by four to one. This animal has no clubs to promote it and no legends or royal connections to enchant the public, but the humble 'moggie' remains the most popular cat worldwide. While some people may have their hearts set on the looks and predictable personality traits of a certain breed, most people are happy to take their chances with whatever specimen happens to steal their heart at the local animal rescue center.

PHYSICAL CHARACTERISTICS
Only a few random-bred cats will have long hair, because it is a recessive trait, but they do occur. Occasionally non-pedigree cats may closely resemble particular breeds, but for the most part they are just reminiscent

of the breeds that emerged from their stock. Type tends to vary from place to place, with stocky, sturdy cats found in cold countries and lighter, more slender cats being more common in warmer climates. However, one is unlikely to find any of the extremes that were selectively bred into the pedigree animals. Random-bred cats tend to be robust and healthy because natural selection ensures survival of the fittest.

Because the white spotting gene is dominant, bi-colors are common in domestic cats. Reds vary in distribution from area to area within most countries and can help to indicate whether adjacent cat populations are interbreeding or not.

Blue is a common color in many areas of mainland Europe. North European cats tend to have small amounts of white in their coats, while in southern Europe white patterns, reminiscent of the Turkish Van, are more common. Without selective breeding, polygenic factors have a large influence on the coat.

TEMPERAMENT

A cat's personality depends on its early experiences, so a random-bred cat is as friendly as one makes it, although it may not achieve the chattiness of Orientals or the placidity of long-haired breeds. Some will be very intelligent, most are assertive, and any cat will remain playful for as long as its owner plays with it.

Above: *Because the white spotting gene is dominant, bi-colors are common.*

DOMESTIC SHORTHAIR

Above: *Typically large, wide-set, but upright ears on a slender head with narrow muzzle.*

Despite its exotic name, this breed did not originate in Cuba. It was first bred in Britain in 1952, where breeders developed a cat of Siamese type with a solid chocolate-colored coat. That specific color was called Havana, but the breed was registered in Britain as Chestnut Brown Foreign.

They were exported to the United States in the mid-1950s. Chestnut Brown Foreigns continued to be imported into America and

Above: *While elegant and graceful, the Havana Brown is a very physical breed and a good climber.*

registered as Havana Browns until 1973, when the Cat Fanciers' Association accepted the Oriental Shorthair breed. From then on these imports were registered as Chestnut Oriental Shorthairs. Ironically, the Oriental Shorthair color, called Chestnut in North America, is now called Havana in Britain, leading to some confusion.

PHYSICAL CHARACTERISTICS

Elegant and graceful, the Havana Brown is an excellent climber. Although this breed's origins are the same as those of the Oriental Shorthair, it was developed to resemble the Russian Blue. The Havana Brown stands high on its legs and is heavy for its size. Kittens and young adults have ghost tabby markings that disappear with age, leaving an even, rich shade of brown. The ears are large and wide-set, but upright. The eyes are oval in shape and green. The head is long and slender, with a narrow muzzle. The whiskers must be brown or lilac to complement the coat color. The body is of medium length and should be carried level. The tail is of medium length and thickness, tapering at the tip. Paws are oval and compact.

TEMPERAMENT

They are very affectionate and loving, sweet and sociable. They are also attention-seeking, and can become demanding. They are curious and learn to open cupboards. They tend to be energetic and good climbers.

Above: *The Havana Brown stands high on its legs and is heavy for its size.*

▶ MAINE COON ◀

One of the largest domestic cats, it is probably descended from the first domestic cats brought to America by the early settlers. It has adapted to survive the hostile winters of New England, where the breed has existed for more than 100 years. A popular household pet and working farm cat, it became well known on the show bench in the late 19th century. However, the popularity of this breed declined as European breeds gained favor. In 1953 a club was formed to promote the breed, which was soon after recognized by the Cat Fanciers Association (CFA) in the United States. It is now recognized in many other countries, as is the very similar Norwegian Forest Cat.

PHYSICAL CHARACTERISTICS

A semi-longhaired cat of medium Foreign type, distinguished by its large size, rectangular appearance, and flowing coat. The head is of medium length, with a square muzzle and firm chin. They have fairly full cheeks with high cheekbones and a nose of uniform width with a shallow, concave curve at the bridge. The ears are large and

Above: *Maine Coon cats usually have tufted ears like this brown tabby.*

BREEDS

Above: *Red and white kitten showing off the Maine Coon's double coat.*

tall, wide at the base, tapering to appear pointed at the tip, which is feathered, and preferably tufted.

The eyes are full and round, spaced wide apart with a slightly oblique aperture. The eye color must be in shades of green, gold, or copper and need not necessarily relate to the coat color. Odd or blue eyes are permissible in white cats.

The body is solid and muscular, of large to medium size, with a broad chest and moderately long neck that is thick and muscular in mature males. The back is long, with a square rump. The limbs are proportionate in length to give the body an overall, and characteristic, rectangular appearance. The legs are substantial with large, round paws, the latter having long tufts of fur extending backwards to create a snowshoe effect. The tail is long, wide at the base, tapering towards the tip, with profuse, long, flowing fur. The coat is waterproof and virtually self-maintaining. The coat is in fact double, with an undercoat covered by a more substantial glossy topcoat. It is shorter on the head, neck and shoulders, increasing in length down the back, flanks, and tail. Breeches and belly fur are full and shaggy. The frontal ruff begins at the base of the ears and is heavier in males. All coat colors and patterns are recognized.

TEMPERAMENT

This is an affectionate, gentle-natured cat with an endearing personality. It is also an alert and capable hunter.

▶ MANX ◀

Above: *Two Manx Torties with tabby-and-white markings indulge in some mutual grooming.*

This is the cat without a tail. It also has the shortest body of all domestic breeds. This breed resulted from a spontaneous mutation that eliminated the vertebrae that form the tail. The origins are uncertain, although they are associated with, and derive their name from, the Isle of Man, which is situated in the Irish Sea. One theory is that the ancestors of today's cats reached the island from the galleons of the Spanish Armada that were sunk by Sir Francis Drake. Others believe that they are descendants of the British Shorthair. However they arrived, their relative isolation on the island ensured that their tailless trait, caused by a dominant gene, was perpetuated. In Britain a Manx club was formed in 1901

and the breed was also shown in the United States early in the 20th century. The traditional Manx was less round than today.

There are long-haired and short-haired versions of the Manx. The Long-haired Manx was developed in North America during the 1960s from long-haired kittens that regularly occurred in litters from the short-haired Manx. They were given the name Cymric (pronounced Kum-ric), which is derived from *Cymru*, the Welsh name for Wales.

Manx litters are usually small and suffer from a high proportion of stillbirths or deaths soon after birth. A litter will often contain a variety of kittens, some without tails, others with tail lengths varying from small knobs to stubby or shortened tails, and tails up to normal length. The true show Manx is tailless, and known as a Rumpy. A Manx with a small tail knob is called a Rumpy-riser; one with a very short tail is called a Stubby or Stumpy; and one with a shortened tail is called a Longy.

The popularity of the Manx has declined in Britain, but they are still shown in the USA.

PHYSICAL CHARACTERISTICS

The Manx is a tailless, short-bodied cat with a rabbity, hopping gait. The head is round and large, but not snubby or of Persian type. The nose is slightly long, with prominent cheeks. The ears are rather wide at the base, tapering off to a point. Eye color is usually of secondary consideration, but when taken into account, it follows the standard set for the British Shorthair: blue for white varieties and amber or orange for other colors. The body comprises a short back with deep flanks. The hind quarters must be as high as possible and the rump rounded. There should be a definite hollow at the end of the backbone, where an ordinary cat's tail would begin. The coat is double, with a longer outer coat and soft, thick undercoat, like that of a rabbit. All colors are recognized, but are only taken into account when all other points are equal.

TEMPERAMENT

The Manx has a calm and gentle disposition. It is affectionate to owners, but may be suspicious of strangers. It can be active, though is not a good climber because it lacks a tail for balance.

Above: *All colors are recognized, since the Manx's defining characteristic is the absent tail.*

▶ NORWEGIAN FOREST CAT ◀

Despite its wild-sounding name, this breed has existed in Norway in domesticated form for centuries. It proved an excellent farm cat and household pet. Its origins are obscure, but certainly resulted from a process of natural selection in the cold, often harsh climate which produces a strong, hardy cat with a thick double coat. Interest in the breed for show purposes started in the 1930s. It is very similar to the Maine Coon, which developed as a farm cat in the New England region.

PHYSICAL CHARACTERISTICS

A large, strong, semi-longhaired cat with a distinctive double coat that dries quickly.

The head is triangular, with a long, straight profile and strong chin. The ears are set high and open, wide at the base, with long hairs protruding from the openings and lynx-like tufts at the tips. The eyes are large, slightly oblique and all colors are allowed. The body is big, long, and strong. The hind legs are longer than the front. The tail is long and bushy.

Above: *The Norwegian Forest cat has much in common with the Maine Coon* (see p170).

Above: *Silver is the result of a white undercoat and color tips.*

The coat is semi-long, consisting of a woolly undercoat covered by a smooth, water-repellent, glossy topcoat that covers the back and sides. A fully coated cat has a shirt-front, full ruff and knickerbockers. In summer the coat is considerably shorter. All coat colors and patterns are recognized, with the exception of Chocolate, Lilac, and the Siamese pattern.

FAULTS (FEATURES FOR WHICH A CAT OF THIS BREED WOULD BE PENALIZED AT A SHOW)
Short tail or legs; round or square head; small ears; small or delicate build.

TEMPERAMENT
This is an intelligent cat, with an affectionate, playful and endearing nature. It is naturally cautious. It is an excellent hunter, and an active, independent outdoor cat that is not recommended for life in a small apartment.

Above: *The Norwegian Forest Cat's build and coat texture are the defining characteristics, not color or pattern.*

▶ ORIENTAL SHORTHAIR ◀

Above: *This Oriental Cinnamon Tabby shows the classic 'foreign' body type.*

More than a century ago, in the early days of showing Siamese, the occasional self-colored (one solid color) kitten with eyes that were not blue was shown in the Siamese class. At the end of the 1920s, however, the Siamese Club of Britain decreed that all Siamese cats should have blue eyes, and interest in the self-colored 'foreign' cats declined. In the 1950s breeders again started to experiment by crossing Siamese with various Shorthairs, particularly the British and American varieties. In 1952 a British breeder produced an all-brown kitten by mating a Siamese with a black Shorthair. This was first called the Havana Brown and then the Oriental Chocolate Cat. In 1958, it was given the name Chestnut Brown Foreign Shorthair. Later the name reverted to Havana Brown.

Out of all the breeding programs came a variety of other colors of non-pointed cat. In some countries they were given the breed name Foreign and in others, Oriental, but most have now adopted the latter name. There are now over 70 Oriental varieties. In almost all of these the standard specifies green eyes (amber is permitted in the US), the only exception being the blue eyes of the Foreign White, and the blue-eyed and odd-eyed Oriental varieties.

Above: *An Oriental Lavender captured in a moment of flehming (see p69–70).*

PHYSICAL CHARACTERISTICS

In physique and temperament the Oriental is Siamese, but in solid coat colors.

FAULTS (FEATURES FOR WHICH A CAT OF THIS BREED WOULD BE PENALIZED AT A SHOW)

Malocclusion of the mouth; white toe or toes (except in Whites); body color that does not adhere to the standard set for a particular color variety; incorrect eye color; permanent squint in one or both eyes.

TEMPERAMENT

These active and athletic cats are outrageously gregarious. Breeders call them shameless flirts. They are demanding, energetic, playful, affectionate, and sociable, they always require human company. True to their Siamese ancestry, they are devoted and loyal.

Right: *If a cat has stripes, it is a tabby. This Oriental's coat is called Chocolate Lynx.*

▶ PERSIAN (LONGHAIR) ◀

Long-haired cats are thought to have originated in Asia. Specimens were first brought to the West by travelers during the 16th century. They reached Italy first and then France and finally Britain. They were probably from Turkey, for they were commonly called Angora (the old name for Ankara). Later specimens, which came from Persia and Afghanistan, had a longer and denser coat and a more cobby body. As breeding programs developed, the two distinctive types that we know today, the Angora and the Persian, emerged. A book published in 1876 referred to long-haired cats as Asiatic cats. However, breeders were selecting for the more thickly coated and cobby type, increasingly known as the Persian, which was gaining favor over the Angora. By 1901

there were 13 recognized colors, which had increased to 160 varieties by the end of the 20th century.

In Britain the name was changed to Longhair, but many countries have continued to call the breed Persian.

PHYSICAL CHARACTERISTICS

A long-haired cat of cobby type with relatively short legs. A distinctive snub nose makes it appear stern, but this is offset by large round eyes that enhance a sweet expression. The head is round and massive, with a great breadth of skull, round face, with round underlying bone structure, set on a short, thick neck. The nose is short, snub, and broad, with a dip. The cheeks are full, the jaws broad and powerful, the chin

Above: *This color is called Cream and is a dilute form of Red.*

Above: *Longhairs require a lot of grooming. This coat color is called Golden.*

full and well developed. The ears are small, round-tipped, tilted forward, and not unduly open at the base. They are set far apart and low on the head, fitting into (without distorting) the rounded contour of the head. The eyes are round and full, brilliant, set far apart, giving the face a sweet expression. The tail is short, but in proportion to body length, carried without a curve, and at an angle lower than the back. The body is cobby, large or medium in size, set low on the legs. The chest is deep and equally massive across the shoulders and rump, with a short, well-rounded middle piece, and level back. The legs are short, thick and strong.

The coat is long and thick, standing out from the body, of fine texture, glossy and full of life. It is long over the body, but a slight shortening of the coat across the shoulder

area is not uncommon in older kittens when the coat is changing. The ruff is immense and continues in a deep frill between the front legs. The ear and toe tufts are very full.

TEMPERAMENT

It is generally amiable, docile, and good-natured, with a soft voice. The Persian's languid nature has earned it a rather undeserved reputation for laziness.

Right: *The Blue coat color is the result of a dilute form of the Black gene.*

Above: *The Russian Blue has green eyes and an extremely dense coat.*

Known for its silvery blue coat, the Russian's fur is so dense that indentations are left when touched. It is a very old breed and, although its present name suggests that the breed originated in Russia, in the early years of the Cat Fancy it was known by several different names, including Archangel Cat, Spanish Blue, and Maltese. It is said that sailors brought specimens of a blue-coated cat to Britain from the Russian port of Archangel.

The breed was classed as Russian or Foreign Blue in 1912. Although interest in it continued between the two world wars, it had virtually disappeared by 1945. After World War II Scandinavian breeders tried to recreate the breed by crossing a blue Finnish cat with a Siamese. In Britain breeders also crossed Siamese with the few Russian Blues that were left. As a result the breed became distinctly Oriental in type. In 1965 a group of British breeders decided to start a new program aimed at creating the original Russian body type. The breed standard was re-written and Siamese type in the breed was made a fault.

White and black varieties have now been produced and are gaining recognition in some countries. In those countries where the other colors are not recognized, the breed is still called the Russian Blue.

PHYSICAL CHARACTERISTICS

It is an elegant, graceful cat of foreign type with a relatively long tail and unique double coat. The head is a short wedge, with a flat skull. The forehead and nose are straight, forming an angle. The whisker pads are prominent. The eyes are a vivid green, almond-shaped, and set rather wide apart. The ears are large and pointed, wide at the base, and set vertically to the head. The skin of the ears is thick and transparent, with very little fur inside. It is of medium build, the body long in outline and graceful in carriage. The legs are long, the feet small and oval. The tail is fairly long and tapering.

The coat is very soft and extremely dense. Each hair of the blue-gray coat is tipped with silver, causing the coat to shimmer. The silver is more dense at the neck and chest. Coat texture and appearance is the truest criterion of the Russian breed.

FAULTS (FEATURES FOR WHICH A CAT OF THIS BREED WOULD BE PENALIZED AT A SHOW)

White (except in the White variety) or tabby markings. Cobby or heavy build. Square head. Yellow in the eyes. Siamese type.

TEMPERAMENT

A quiet, soft-voiced cat that is rather shy and undemanding, although affectionate to its owners.

Above: *On parts of its body the dense coat is tipped with silver to make it shimmer.*

▶ SIAMESE ◀

Despite various other theories about its origin, this breed really did originate in Siam (now Thailand) many hundreds of years ago. Cats with similar pointed markings feature in the *Cat Book Poems*, a manuscript saved from Ayudha, the old capital of Siam, which was burned down in 1767. It is the best known of a number of manuscripts that provide a record of the native cats, dogs and birds of the region at that time.

The Siamese pattern was later recorded in Russia by the naturalist Simon Pallas, in 1793. However, the cats he encountered were of much darker coloring. This could be explained by the fact that the Siamese points darken in colder climates. It is not known whether the Russian cats were descended from original Siamese imports, or whether the Siamese gene mutation (now commonly known as the Himalayan gene) had occurred naturally in Russia.

Siamese cats were already in Britain before 1871, for in that year they featured at the first National Cat Show in London. There were many stories about their origin and at one time they were labeled as 'an unnatural, nightmare kind of cat.' Nevertheless, their popularity grew and specimens were brought to America around 1890. The body shape of the Siamese has altered considerably over the years as breeders and judges select ever more extreme 'Oriental' type. Breeders have developed a wide variety of coat colors and patterns. The Himalayan gene carried by the Siamese (and other pointed cats) causes dilution of any

Above: *Chocolate Point Siamese. Chocolate is a dilute form of the Black gene.*

Above: *Pointed kittens are light-colored, the darker markings appearing as they mature.*

particular color. Hence there is no black Siamese because the color is diluted to a very dark brown, called Seal. Siamese have also given rise to the Oriental varieties which are, in effect, 'non-pointed' Siamese.

PHYSICAL CHARACTERISTICS

This is a short-haired cat of Oriental type with a long svelte body and an alert, intelligent expression. The head is long and wedge-shaped, neither rounded nor pointed, with width between the eyes narrowing in perfectly straight lines to a fine muzzle. The profile is straight, with a firm chin in line with the upper jaw. The ears are large, well-pricked and wide at the base. The eye shape is Oriental, slanting towards the nose. The eye color is a deep blue. The body is medium in size, long and svelte, with proportionately slim legs. The hind legs are slightly higher than the forelegs, the feet small and oval. The tail is long and tapering. The coat is very short and fine in texture, glossy and close-lying. The mask is completely connected to the ears by tracings. In all colors kittens may not show full masking, nor the adult color on legs and tail.

FAULTS (FEATURES FOR WHICH A CAT OF THIS BREED WOULD BE PENALIZED AT A SHOW)

Green tinge or otherwise incorrect eye color; malocclusion of the mouth; white toe(s); point or body color that does not adhere to the standard set for the particular color; permanent squint in one or both eyes.

TEMPERAMENT

Siamese are extremely affectionate, devoted, and loyal. They are highly intelligent, inquisitive, active, and very vocal. The other side of the coin is that they are also very demanding. These traits may make them unsuitable for some elderly people. Some strains can be temperamental and highly strung.

▶ TURKISH VAN ◀

Above: *The red (called Auburn in this breed) is restricted to the ears and tail.*

Centuries ago a cat population established itself, for reasons unknown, in the area around Lake Van in southeastern Turkey. Because of their isolation, the animals became a distinctive breed. Individuals had a characteristic red-and-white pattern that is rare in other cats. The red (now called auburn) was restricted to areas around the ears and the tail. They seemed to love water and swimming. Although known to the local people, it was not until the 1950s that they were 'discovered' and taken to Britain, where they were recognized as a breed in 1969.

PHYSICAL CHARACTERISTICS

A small to medium-sized, graceful, lithe and well-balanced cat, with a medium-long coat and characteristic red-and-white markings. The head is small to medium, wide at the top, tapering to the chin. Allowance is made for jowls in stud cats. The ears are set high on the head; wide at the base; long; pointed and tufted.

The eyes are large, almond-shaped to round, slanting slightly upwards, colored amber with pink eye rims. They are also sometimes odd-eyed (one eye is blue and

Above: *The dilute of Auburn is Cream, but follows the Van pattern in all other respects.*

the other amber). The nose is medium to long with a gentle slope and no break. The chin is gently rounded, yet firm. The neck is slim, graceful, and of medium length.

The body is fine-boned, small to medium in females, slightly larger in males. The torso is long, graceful, and lithe. The rump is slightly higher than the front. The paws are small, round and dainty, with tufts between the toes and pink paw pads. The tail is long and tapering.

The coat is medium to long, long at the ruff, with a full brush on the tail, but not as full as the Persian. The fur is fine and silky, with a tendency to part, and wavy on the stomach. The body color is white, with spots of auburn on the head and an auburn-ringed tail with even striping. Auburn spots on the back are allowed.

Right: *The Van's soft coat is water resistant and 'breaks' open over curves.*

TEMPERAMENT

It is a placid and good-natured cat; friendly and affectionate towards owners and strangers. It can also be active and playful.

Ailurophobe: a person who dislikes or is afraid of cats.

Alter: neuter (applies to either gender).

Bi-color: a cat with patches of white and any other solid color.

Black: the darkest of all feline colors, which can have a rust appearance during molting.

Blaze: a distinctive, contrasting mark running down a cat's face from forehead to nostrils.

Blotched: a tabby pattern, also known as Classic tabby or Marbled tabby.

Blue: a dilution of black that may vary from a soft gray to a dark slate color.

Breed standard: a written description of what the ideal specimen of a given breed should look like.

Caregiver: person responsible for a pet cat or for a feral colony. These days 'owner' may be considered politically incorrect.

Castrate: to remove the testes (neutering of male cats).

Catnip: a herbaceous plant, similar to mint, to which cats are strongly attracted.

Chocolate: a dark brown coat color.

Cobby: short and sturdy, on low legs.

Cream: the dilute of orange (ginger or red).

De-sex: neuter (applies to either gender).

Dilute: a lighter color variation of a standard cat color.

Domestic: an animal that has become adapted to humans over many generations, and has a genetic predisposition to tameness.

Double coat: two thick coats in one, comprising a soft undercoat of thick, short hairs and another set of coarser, slightly longer hairs.

DSH: Domestic Shorthair. A non-pedigree short-haired cat

Entire: unneutered, unaltered.

Ex-feral: a feral cat that has been tamed and that now lives as a pet.

Feral: an ex-domestic cat that has reverted to being fully wild, or the wild-born (never known domesticity) offspring of stray cats.

Furball: fur swallowed by the cat during self-grooming, which forms into a tightly packed ball in the stomach or bowels. Also known as 'hairball'.

Ghost markings: faint tabby markings seen in some solid-colored coats, especially in kittens.

Inbreeding: mating of closely related cats (siblings, mother/son, father/daughter) to strengthen desirable traits.

Lavender: a dilute of Chocolate, also known as Lilac or Platinum.

Lilac: see Lavender.

Locket: a white spot at the base of a cat's throat.

Mackerel: the pattern of tabby markings in which thin, unbroken lines run vertically down the cat's body from the spine line.

Marbled: see Blotched.

Mask: the darker-colored areas of the face in some cats e.g. Siamese.

Moggy (Moggie): mixed breed, cross-breed or random-bred cat.

Neoteny: the persistence of 'kitten' characteristics in an adult cat.

Neuter: to surgically render sterile; applies to males and females, but is usually used as a euphemism for castration.

Odd-eyed: a cat with one blue eye and one that is green, gold, or copper.

Outbreeding: mating unrelated individuals to improve type or vigor.

Outcrossing: mating a pedigree cat to a cat of a different breed or type in order to improve the breed or to introduce new traits.

Pedigree: cat with a family tree registered with the breed regulatory body. A pedigree cat is not necessarily purebred, since some breeds have allowable outcrosses.

Penciling: the fine lines on the cheeks of tabby cats.

Points: the extremities of a cat's body: the mask, ears, legs, paws, and tail. The points of Siamese cats are darker than the body color.

Purebred: having only individuals of the same breed in its family tree; no outcrossings.

Queen: an unspayed female cat.

Red: coat color caused by the orange gene, found in most breeds of cat.

Self: evenly colored fur of one color, also called solid.

Semi-feral: a non-domestic cat which lives in close proximity to humans and is accustomed to human presence, while remaining wild.

Smoke: a dark topcoat that is white or silver at the roots.

Spay: to remove the ovaries and womb (ovario-hysterectomy).

Spotted: a tabby pattern where the bands are broken into spots.

Sterilize: to neuter (either gender).

Stray: a domestic cat with no home or owner.

Tabby: a coat with dark stripes, spots, or wavy marks on a lighter background.

Ticked: two or three bands of contrasting color on a cat's hair.

Tipped: the contrasting color at the tips of the hairs of some cats' coats.

Tom: a male cat, particularly an uncastrated male cat.

Tortoiseshell: a coat patched or mixed with black and red. Usually a female cat.

Wild: often used to denote a feral cat, but a wild cat is strictly a member of a non-domestic species e.g. European Wildcat.

▶ . INDEX ◀

Note: Page numbers in **bold** refer to all illustrated material.

▶ PHOTOGRAPHIC CREDITS ◀

AL = Alexis; A/JC = Anipix/Jan Castrium;
B = Bios; BC = Bruce Coleman; C = Cogis;
D = Dammon; DVZ = Dries van Zyl;
E&PB = Erwin & Peggy Bauer;
FN = Foto Natura; G = Gissey;
GM = (c) Graham Meadows Ltd,
www.gmphotolibrary.com;
H = Hermeline; HR = Hans Reinhard;
Helmi = Helmi Flick Cat Photography;

JB = Jane Burton; JJ = Johnny Johnson;
KH = Klein-Hubert; KT = Kim Taylor;
L = Lanceau; LH = Leonard Hoffmann;
O = Okapia; PB = Picture Box;
PVG = Paul van Gaalen;
RC = R Cavinaux; RM = Robert Maier;
SIL = Struik Image Library;
ST = Sally-Anne Thompson;
V = Vidal; WP = Warren Photographic.

(Abreviations: t=top;		31	WP/JB	64	ST	108	GM
b=bottom; r=right;		32	GM	66	BC/JB	110	KH/FN
l=left)		33	BC/JB	67	BC/HR	111(t)	ST
1	WP/JB	34	WP/JB	68	WP/JB	111(b)	BC/KT
2	WP/JB	35	WP/JB	69	WP/JB	112	GM
4–5	PB	36	WP/JB	70	GM	113	C/L
6–7	WP/JB	37(t)	GM	71	BC/KT	114(t)	GM
8	WP/JB	37(b)	GM	73	WP/JB	114(b)	WP/JB
10	GM	38	PB	74	BC/JB	115	GM
11	BC/E&PB	39	BC/HR	75	BC/JB	116	WP/JB
12(t)	WP/JB	40	C/H	76	BC/JB	117	GM
12(b)	GM	41(t)	BC/HR	77	BC/JB	119	GM
13(t)	BC/JB	41(b)	WP/JB	78	BC/JB	132	GM
13(b)	WP/JB	42	WP/JB	81	C/D	133	SIL
14	WP/JB	43(l)	WP/JB	82	BC/JB	134	GM
15	WP/JB	43(r)	WP/JB	83	JC/FN	135	GM
16	GM	44	ST	84	A/JC	136	KH/O/FN
17(t)	GM	45	A/JC	85	PB	137	RC/B/FN
17(b)	GM	46(t)	BC/RM	86	WP/JB	138	GM
18	ST	46(l)	WP/JB	87	WP/JB	139	KH/B/FN
19	A/JC	46(r)	A/JC	88(t)	BC	143	SIL/LH
20	C/H	47	C/H	88(b)	WP/JB	144–145	C/G
21	C/H	48	WP/JB	89	BC	148–151	GM
22	BC/HR	50	C/V	90	WP/JB	152	Helmi
24	C/AL	51	C/H	92	A/JC	153	Alan Robinson
25(t)	GM	52	WP/JB	93	GM	154–159	GM
25(b)	GM	54	SIL	94	GM	160	Helmi
26(t)	ST	55	SIL	95	WP/JB	161–165	GM
26(b)	WP/JB	57	SIL	96	WP/JB	166 Geraldine Cupido	
27(t)	GM	58	GM	98	WP/JB	167(t)	GM
27(b)	ST	59(l&r)	SIL	101	WP/JB	167(b)Nicholas Aldridge	
28	WP/JB	60	ST	102	GM	168–169	Helmi
29(t)	ST	61	SIL	105	GM	170–185	GM
29(b)	BC/JB	62(t&b)	SIL	106	A/JC	Cover,	
30	BC/JB	63	SIL	107	A/JC	including spine	WP/JB